The
Day
Calendar

A Baby Boomer's Memoir

Tom Shropshire

ISBN: 978-0-9968721-1-9

Table of Contents

Foreword: Moments to Remember 1

Childhood: The Fifties – The Early Years 3

Childhood: The Fifties – The Middle Years 27

Jr High School – Late Fifties, Early Rock & Roll 64

High School: 1960 – The Big Time 78

High School: 1963 – The Awakening 105

In Limbo – Between High School and the Navy 122

In the Navy – Boston to Bangkok 134

To Viet Nam and Home Again 182

Acknowledgements 209

Foreword: Moments to Remember

This book is a memoir. A tale of growing up as a "baby boomer" in Aurora, Illinois, and of my experiences in those times which now seem to have come, and gone, so quickly.

From the distance of now more than 60 years, much of my childhood, and beyond, is a hodgepodge of clear, and sometimes not so clear, recollections. As with most people I suppose, music is a powerful memory trigger, and so, as I gathered and wrote these recollections, I occasionally referenced the music and the songs of which I was fond at the time, and which brought back to me many of the memories I offer here.

All through my adolescence and well beyond, like most of my peers I was dedicated to popular music, experienced mostly through the speakers of a portable record player, or an AM radio – often in the dashboard of a car, or from a transistor radio pressed to my ear.

But even in early childhood, music was everywhere, from my mother's phonograph console, to the large Philco radio in the den, to the variety shows and *Your Hit Parade* on early TV. So, even in childhood, the music of the adult world was mine as well.

It seems only fitting, therefore, that I begin this memoir with lines from a very popular song, which I recall from my ninth year – "Moments to Remember" by the Four Lads:

"Though summer turns to winter
And the present disappears
The laughter we were glad to share
Will echo through the years
When other nights and other days
May find us gone our separate ways
We will have these moments to remember"

"Moments To Remember" by Al Stillman and Robert Allen
Published by Larry Spier Music LLC, New York, NY.
Printed with permission. All rights reserved.

Childhood: The 1950s – The Early Years

Introduction: Recalling the Baby Boomers' Era

While the European portion of the Second World War ended in May of 1945, it looked as though the campaign against Japan would go on for some time. "The Golden Gate in '48" was a popular phrase among Pacific Fleet sailors at the time. So, in August of 1945, it came as something of a surprise when hostilities in the Pacific abruptly ended, and the urgent need to transfer personnel from Europe to the Pacific for the final assault on the Japanese home islands became unnecessary. Not only were units from Europe no longer needed, but most of the forces in the Pacific theater had suddenly become superfluous, as well.

Obviously, an alternative plan was called for, and so, one was quickly developed. With priority based upon points earned for time in service, battles attended, age, family status, etc., the GIs, marines, sailors, airmen, doctors, nurses, and the rest were instead shipped home to get started on the baby boom.

One small result of all this was me. I was born at St. Charles Hospital in Aurora, Illinois in early October of 1946 and therefore consider myself to be a charter member of the baby boom generation.

Like every generation, before and after, the baby boomers grew and experienced many distinct and historically unique events. The flying saucer sightings of the mid-fifties, and the 1956 election campaign, "I Like Ike," were followed by hula-hoops, and Sputnik, and "The Chipmunk Song."

The "sixties" began with JFK, the "New Frontier," and a small, faraway civil war of seemingly little consequence. After a traumatic and profound societal shift, the era continued with LBJ, the "Great Society," and the War. The era ended with Richard Nixon, the counterculture and the underground, Neil Armstrong's small step onto the moon, and of course, the WAR.

After the high of the sixties, the antithetical 1970s seem to have passed in something of a blur. I recall the gas shortage, streaking, a 1950s revival craze, and not much else of any real significance, other than my relocation to Milwaukee in 1975, and of course, the Carter years which thankfully gave way to Reagan's eighties.

This narrative, part one of my overall journey, is a chronicle of my passage through those sometimes prosaic, sometimes turbulent years – from my first memories, to my return home from Viet Nam and the US Navy in 1967 – as seen and experienced by the person I was at the time, and recalled by the ever-changing person I am yet coming to be.

Bill Cosby titled one of his early comedy albums, *I Started Out as a Child*. Well, me too. Actually, I know I started out somewhere prior to childhood, but since I have as little recollection of my infancy as I have of the American Civil War, childhood seems a pretty good place to begin.

The Day Calendar

I remember in my grade school years wishing, as perhaps all children do, that I were older, with the curious insight of being aware of myself as a child in a mostly adult world, with a seemingly endless lifetime ahead. I would sometimes envision a day calendar, with pages falling away as they did in the movies to suggest the passage of time. I would imagine myself older, able to do the things adults could do, but with no knowledge of the adult world, or any anticipation of the teen years that would take me there. But I felt a sort of pull, wanting to move the process along.

Real time, when you are eight, or nine, or ten, grinds forward with an aching slowness. The interminable, almost endless school year, followed by the sheer timelessness of summer, made life's milestones – Christmases, birthdays, the last day of each school year, the 4th of July fireworks – always come as something of a surprise that it was actually "THE Day."

But a year in those days marked the passing of roughly ten percent of one's whole life, and so, perspective was limited. How strange to remember seeing – in my mind's eye – the pages of that calendar falling away, so that weeks, and months, and even years passed in a blur. And to realize after all, that that is just what has happened.

Venturing Forth –
Beginning the Grade School Experience

My initial memory continues to be my first day at kindergarten – specifically, of our teacher introducing us to the school's Patrol Boys!! The equal opportunity concept of Patrol Girls still lay several years in the future.

I missed much of what was said about these patrol people, however, because upon hearing the term, I immediately associated Patrol Boys with Space Patrol, or some such. In the fall of 1951, science fiction was just coming into its heyday, you see, and I found it perfectly logical to think that these Patrol Boys were there to take us on trips to outer space. My first thought, as I recall, was, "Oh boy! They're going to take us on a trip to the moon!"

It's sad looking back only to realize that my very first memory is of something that turned out to be a complete disappointment. Patrol Boys, it was revealed, were just kids, a few years older, who saw to it that you crossed the street without getting squashed by the Lincoln Avenue bus. Heck, I was five years old – I already knew how to do *that*.

One reason I knew, and would continue to know, about buses, and cars, and all the rest, was that early in September of each year the local newspaper, *The Aurora Beacon News*, ran a full-page picture of automobile skid marks and a child's lunchbox with lunch – sandwich, banana, and cookie – scattered on the pavement. The large caption for this read, "Johnny Won't Be Going to School This Year."

Childhood is tough, and part of the dues is having adults scare the bejesus out of you at every opportunity. I must grant, however, that the point was made.

Childhood Music

I don't remember too much of the music of those very early years, except for "The Teddy Bear's Picnic" and "Captain Jinks of the Horse Marines" who, we are told, feeds his horse on pork and beans, and oh yes, the ballad of "Old Shep."

This last was about a boy, Jim, and his ever faithful companion. The ending, a sort of doggy euthanasia, never failed to set me bawling when my mother sang the song to me. Even now when I think of it I get a little misty, though probably more for the lost innocence and simplicity of the boy I was, than for the fate of a fictional dog.

Ghosts of Christmas Past

Among the good memories, which counterpoint the initial disappointment, was Christmas. The season was, of course, magical; the waiting both agonizing and delicious, the weather in those days almost always cold and snowy. At school, in art class – my favorite – we made paper chains, and drawings of holly, and bells, and candles, and combinations of the above to decorate our otherwise drab classroom. At home, the tree was always spectacular. Dad always found the best tree, full and fragrant, and Mother was a true artist at trimming. Our tree was always the best.

Sometimes, I would slide under the tree and lay on my back, looking up through the lights, and tinsel, and ornaments. The colored lights created a glow and the warmth released the aroma of the pine, and there I would lie, enthralled by the vision which became, for those moments, the entire universe.

Even in the lean years Santa was good to us, and Christmas morning, *early*, was always all it could be. Christmas Eve, and after about noontime on Christmas Day, were always spent at Grandma's house with the family – the Shropshires, the Drakes, Aunt Mary (and for a while, Uncle Luigi), and of course, Grandma. Lots of snacks, the intra-family gift exchange, followed by coffee and Christmas cookies, was the Christmas Eve agenda. Then home to await Santa.

At the mid-point of my first decade, I was the only grandchild, and for a few more years, there were only infants and toddlers, so I was somewhat doted upon. This changed, of course, as my siblings, David and Mary, and cousins, John and Donald, grew. Surprisingly, this was okay with me for I now had peers, more or less, with whom I could share the experience.

On one of those early Christmas Eves, I was paid a visit by Santa Claus himself – a rare treat and privilege, I know. But, for reasons known only to him, and perhaps some elves, he decided to personally deliver my first two-wheel bicycle. I could not have been more thrilled and awed. It was suggested, some years later, that it was really my uncle's brother, but to this moment, in my heart, I *know* – it really was Santa

Volcanoes and Captain Video

A major reason why I did not become a geologist, aside from my lifelong aversion to any academic exertion, is that at about age five or six, I was badly frightened by, of all things, volcanoes. They had for me an almost supernatural aura, characterized by the ability, so I feared at the time, to appear literally out of nowhere.

For most of my grade school years, I had an occasionally reoccurring nightmare of a volcano erupting inside a garage as I was walking home from school. Just as I was passing by a house on Lincoln Avenue, between Bardwell School and the old hospital cafeteria, the garage at the end of the driveway would explode as the volcano inside let go. I can still, yes even now, conjure images of chunks of splintered board and garage parts flying through the air. Immediately after the explosion, I would wake up, so I never knew the result of this extraordinary occurrence.

But I do know now, as I knew then, what caused this fear. It came from watching what was at the time, a very popular TV program. Ultimately determined to be a terrible program for children to view, *Captain Video and His Video Rangers* was nonetheless a favorite of adults.

For three serial episodes, the "rangers" were trapped on a planet, awaiting the inevitable rescue by Captain Video. The surface of the planet was *all* volcanoes; and viewing their terror, supplemented by the many close camera shots of bubbling lava (actually it was Malt-O-Meal, I think) scared me pretty badly. But the grown-ups liked the show; one of the few things on TV at the time which wasn't wrestling or roller derby, and I was, I guess, too dumb not to look.

Saturday Nights at Aunt Goldie's: Part 1

In my earlier grade school years, there was a time when I spent quite a few Saturday evenings at a large, crowded house in Montgomery, which I knew as "Aunt Goldie's." Goldie Edwards was my father's older sister. She and her husband, Henry, lived in a big old house on South Lake Street with their many children, ranging from my age to the oldest, Cousin Bob, who was a grown-up; old enough, in fact, to own his own blacktop paving business.

It was a custom for a while that my parents, with Aunt Goldie and Uncle Henry, would spend Saturday evenings at Shannon's Tap in "downtown" Montgomery. In the early 1950s, I'm sure this represented the authentic old-time honky-tonk experience. My father didn't listen to music all that much, but I know he liked the contemporary country singers, particularly Hank Snow, whom I have no doubt was well represented on the juke-box. In the meantime, I got to spend a fun evening with my cousins. Those not out on a date were either in my age range, or old enough to babysit.

We always left for Aunt Goldie's at about 6:15 on Saturday evening, right in the middle of *Beat the Clock*, a hugely popular TV show, hosted by Bud Collyer. Contestants vied for prizes by performing moderately difficult and visually hilarious tasks, usually involving whipped cream or water, within a prescribed time, usually one minute. Time was ticked off by the large clock for which the show was named. Sound familiar?

The concept has been expanded and proliferated to ridiculous extremes, but in its day, *Beat the Clock* was amusing and entertaining, especially for the small boy I was then.

It seemed that always, at the most critical moment, it was "time to go to Aunt Goldie's," and by the time we got there, the show was, of course, over. But I quickly forgot about it as I got together with my cousins. While watching their older siblings, the teenagers, prepare to go out on dates and such, we eagerly planned the evening's fun.

Saturday Nights at Aunt Goldie's: Part 2 – Dining Room Table Submarine

It is remarkable just how much of our play, as children in the 1950s, was related to, or inspired by, the Second World War. On second thought, I guess it's not so surprising after all, for late-night television programming of the era was full of WWII films, and a number of regular entertainment programs were war-themed as well.

We grew up with not only Howdy Doody, Sky King, and the Mouseketeers, but with *Combat* (infantry in Europe), *Silent Service* (submarines in the Pacific), *12 O'Clock High* (bombers over Europe), and a host of others. And perhaps most importantly, nearly all of our fathers, and uncles, and in many cases, older brothers and cousins, had served somewhere during the war, only 10 years or so prior, and so I suspect we felt the need to vicariously share their experience.

My cousins and I at Aunt Goldie's were a mixed group of boys *and* girls, and one of our favorite group activities was to turn the large dining room table into a submarine for the purpose of sinking Japanese ships. Chairs placed upside down on the table with backs hanging down over the sides, plus cushions from the living room couch created a darkened, cramped space beneath the table, magically transforming it into just the kind of WWII submarine we had seen on TV, and in which we crept through dangerous waters, torpedoed enemy ships, and survived devastating depth charge attacks.

As the night progressed, exhausted by our valiant efforts, we began to grow a little sleepy, but my older cousin(s) made sure we disassembled our submarine before we dozed off, content with the feeling that we had done our part to win the war.

The Bomb

I have often heard how we were all somehow psychologically damaged, growing up under the shadow of "The Bomb." While this may have been true for the deep thinkers among us – of whom I and my peers were definitely not – I witnessed little evidence of it.

Unlike our elders of draft age, who it seems were obsessed by it. By the time *we* were old enough to be aware, atomic bombs were established reality, and I for one never believed that anyone, of any political or ideological persuasion, was dumb enough to do such a thing as to actually launch one (or more). So, without knowing it, I was a believer in Ike's MAD (Mutually Assured Destruction) policy which, as it turned out, was quite effective.

As for the accidental trigger, à la Dr. Strangelove, or as we have since learned, the Cuban Missile Crisis, yes, the danger was there, but a necessary evil associated with the weapons which had, in fact, kept us safe. In our daily lives, the possibility of an auto accident, or for a while the very real possibility of contracting polio were far more conscious concerns.

Looking back, it was teenagers, college students, and academics – who *were* prone to think deep thoughts – having lived theretofore in a "atomic-free" world who seemed to actively fear the Bomb, and who were obsessed with the notion of organizing to save the world from an otherwise inevitable doom.

The ubiquitous peace symbol of the sixties era was, in fact, the 1950s concatenation of the semaphore signals for the letters N and D (the symbol for the Campaign for Nuclear Disarmament designed by Gerald Holtom in 1958), which was usurped by the next generation as the universal symbol for peace and love.

Pony Rides

In the early 1950s, there were pony rides in Phillips Park. Located on the circle drive, a bit past the WWI cannons and roughly across from where the jet fighter would later be parked, was a small bridle path, a fenced oval about 50 yards or so in diameter, with a gate and a ticket stand.

There was a man who sold tickets and who was generally in charge. Also around were teenagers, hired to walk the ponies, and of course, their riders. As I recall, a ticket purchased a lap, with a total duration of about 10 minutes. This is a fair amount of time when you are eight years old, but is also sadly over far too quickly when you're on horseback.

My father took me one evening, as a surprise, for a ride on the ponies. He paid the man, I happily mounted the pony, and off I went on my adventure. What I did not know at the time was that the ticket-taker was a workplace friend of my father's. So, as the man took tickets and directed operations, he and my father chatted. When my lap was completed, the man told the boy leading my pony to "take him around again." So, to my delight, off I went for another lap.

I couldn't imagine, nor did I care, what the conversation was about, but I'm sure the man was happy for the diversion and it was a pleasant evening, so the scene was repeated several times, and I stayed "pony-back" for well over half an hour.

All in all, a great evening, and surely the best experience I've ever had with a horse (as sometime later it would seem that all the horses in the world got together and decided they didn't like me). So, I will always cherish the memory of that hour of excitement and pure joy.

Learning to Color

Sometime in my earlier years at Bardwell Elementary School, I realized that I could draw, paint, and cut paper, and was generally more artistic than many of my little classmates. When I was perhaps seven or eight years old, I remember learning to color. Prior to that day, like every other little kid, I couldn't stay inside the lines of my coloring book.

Suddenly, while coloring with my friend Ricky Jensen on his

living room floor, I discovered the secret. If I first outlined the area I wanted to fill in, keeping inside the lines was no problem. No matter that I had simply traced over lines already printed on the page; they were boundaries *that I had drawn for myself,* and staying within them was not so hard at all.

While the moral of this tale would lurk below the level of my consciousness for many years, the benefits of this incipient artistic ability were more immediate. I now had one area of my grade school experience in which I not only didn't fall short of expectations, but actually exceeded them.

During art period, I could show off when asked to display my renderings before an awed and admiring class. This made up, if temporarily, for being humiliated in front of these same classmates almost daily for not finishing my arithmetic homework. The questionable concept of outcome-based education still lay well in the future. In the 1950s, being ridiculed in front of your classmates was considered a sound motivational tool.

Learning to Color (Part II – The Downside)

There was a downside to my burgeoning artistic ability, however. It turned out that my ability and desire to draw things in which I was interested – WWII planes, ships, speedboats, and other things – or sometimes just doodling patterns and shapes – led to trouble when done in any classroom time that was *not* art period.

These efforts, some quite good I must say given my age, unfortunately often appeared in the margins of grammar or arithmetic worksheets which I had to turn in to the teacher. Regardless of the level of success I achieved in completing the assignment, these doodlings were always mistakenly interpreted as prima facie evidence that I was not paying attention in class. This, of course, led to an inevitable series of results; ridicule in class, a trip to see the principal – the altogether frightening Miss Lonergan – and, of course, notes to my parents.

After a while, I wised up to a degree, and did my doodling on my own paper.

Thoughts about Snakes

I don't like snakes! In fact, to say that I fear snakes, or have a snake phobia, is an understatement on the order of saying that the sky is a place above your head. I have a monumental phobia about creatures that have no legs, and to a lesser degree, creatures with too many legs, but that's another matter. I received this fear from, of all people, my mother.

When I was small, my mother and I would often go to visit my grandmother, and in those days if we had a car at all, my father drove it to work. So we walked. It was a journey of just over two miles from our house, across the Fox River to Grandma's, and the EJ&E (Elgin, Joliet, & Eastern) Railroad Bridge was directly in line between the two points.

There was a narrow, wooden plank walkway beside the tracks so pedestrians could also use the bridge. On the eastern side, a wide, level, gravel pathway lead from South Broadway to the bridge, while on the western side, the flood plain, the tracks continued on an artificial ridge while a narrow, overgrown path descended for about 50 yards from the bridge to South River Street. It was on this stretch that my mother would constantly warn me to, "Watch out for snakes."

I can't blame her though. She had an experience when she was little that would have had me in therapy for years. She and her two sisters were running home from an errand to Prisco's Italian Grocery Store, and were about to run up onto their terraced front lawn when one of my future aunts yelled, "Olga, look out!" On the lawn, just in front of her, was a particularly nasty-looking snake. At eight years old, my mother was not very tall, and at the foot of the terrace, she was eye to eye with the creature.

She then did just what I would do, even today. She reversed course and ran screaming to the backyard where my grandfather, as luck would have it, was working in the garden with a hoe.

As her father marched, hoe in hand, to the front, my mother ran inside the back door of the house. After a couple of nervous minutes, she summoned the courage to creep to the front door and peek out through the glass. The snake, having meanwhile crawled onto the front porch, peeked back at her.

This double whammy gave her the phobia which I possess to this day. She was, as it turned out, very fortunate. The snake was determined to be a viper of some kind which, the neighborhood speculated, must have crawled onto a Burlington Route freight car in the southwest somewhere and dropped off the train as it rumbled through the "South End" of Aurora on its way to Chicago. Very scary stuff indeed.

Daily Adventures

© Louis Cerney

I think we were a lot more independent as kids than is generally true today. You can argue that it is a more dangerous world now, and I won't disagree. But I will suggest that our childhood world had its perils – they were just different. And although I believe society is now more dangerous for children, the world, the physical environment in which we as kids entertained ourselves, was fraught with peril, as it was not overly encumbered with fences, barriers, and warning signs. Litigation being what it was in the 1950s, we were mostly free to explore, enter, climb over, and routinely take risks which are simply not available today. Couple this with the fact that our days, in summer anyway, were unorganized and almost entirely unsupervised. We had few, if any, of the planned "activities" by which today's children expect to be entertained.

The summer weekday, and many Saturdays as well, started with breakfast – a bowl of corn flakes (Kellogg's, of course), or Wheaties, Cheerios, Rice Krispies (Snap, Crackle, and Pop), or whatever was your favorite.

There weren't too many pre-sweetened cereals in those days.

There was Raisin Bran, Puffed Wheat, the multi-colored, and supposedly multi-flavored Trix (Raspberry RED, Lemon YELLOW, Orange ORANGE), and of course, Tony the Tiger never let us forget that Frosted Flakes were Grrrrrreat.

Being a fairly typical child of the fifties, after breakfast, if there was no school, I would often just disappear until lunchtime. Summer days were mostly a series of random, and unplanned, events. My bicycle – sometimes with neighbor, Billy Elliot, riding on the back – would take me anywhere I wanted to go around the eastside of Aurora, and sometimes beyond. We roamed far and wide, from various parks, to downtown, to the railroad bridge over the Fox River which was, for several reasons, a favorite destination.

The EJ&E Railroad Bridge crossed the Fox River about a mile from our house. The solid green vegetation around and below the bridge was a close enough approximation to our vision of the jungles of the South Pacific. We fought and defeated many imaginary Japanese soldiers in that swampy, sweaty green. The bridge structure itself, and the shallow rapids of the river at that spot, looked to me very much like the movie version of *The Bridge on the River Kwai*, which greatly enhanced the fun. Oddly enough, this is the very place at which I received, from my mother, my phobia of snakes. But when we were fighting the Japs, I didn't give it a thought.

The bridge also offered a different kind of fun. From the pedestrian walkway tacked to the side of the span, you could – with no warning signs, fences, or guard rails to protect us from the 40-foot drop – cross over to the tracks and climb down onto the center support, the top surface of which was perhaps four feet below the track supporting ties. This offered a very private space, a great view of the river, and much excitement when a train thundered by just inches above our heads.

Lunchtime – Soup, Tuna, and Kool-Aid

No matter where we would travel to on summer mornings when I was a kid, when lunchtime rolled around, I would always somehow manage to show up at home just in time for the noon meal – usually a tuna salad sandwich, a bowl of Campbell's soup (chicken noodle, please), and Kool-Aid. My mother once said she wouldn't have made it through raising children without these three staples.

During the school year, because I lived only two blocks from Bardwell Elementary School, I always came home for lunch. I was occasionally joined by one or another of my grade school friends, Clifford Allen, Mark Seibers, or David Larson (or sometimes to one of their houses too, of course, for pretty much exactly the same fare).

While eating, we were usually entertained by Uncle Johnny Coons (NBC-Channel 5 in Chicago), or Two Ton Baker (The Music Maker) (ABC-Channel 7). Bozo the Clown (WGN-Channel 9) had not yet made an appearance, and what we didn't know, we didn't miss. Uncle Johnny was my favorite, but ol' Two Ton was okay. Dressed in costume, he played a piano on the deck of a pirate ship and interacted with comical crew members and various sea creatures, including Bubbles the Porpoise, who apparently lived alongside the ship.

One thing I recall about those lunches, my friend David – son of a doctor and *perhaps* a bit more sophisticated for his age than I – would nonetheless laugh wildly at these shows with his mouth fully open, regardless of the half-chewed sandwich parts within. But he was my pal, so I ignored it (mostly).

After lunch, it was back to school; or in summer, back to the streets, looking for whatever might capture our interest until it was time for dinner.

Evenings Closer to Home

In the timeless summers of my grade school years, we would spend our days roaming far and wide through the streets of Aurora. But after dinner, we stayed closer to home. Neighborhood kids of more diverse ages, with whom you might not interact during the day, would gather and think of something to do until it got dark.

It seems that it was in the evenings, with the neighborhood kids, that we most often played "Cowboys and Indians." We could usually muster up the appropriate number of cap guns and bow and arrow sets, though someone occasionally had to resort to a pointed finger and a heartily yelled "Bang!" But cap pistols were better; they made a satisfactory sound, and the smoke smelled pretty good.

As for the Indians, the only arrows available were, of course, equipped with suction cup tips. This was not satisfactory at all. Suction cup arrows are not very aerodynamic, and will not only not fly true, they will also not fly very far. The simple and obvious solution to this was to remove the suction cups. Problem solved – the arrows would now fly straight, true, and pretty far.

I know this first hand, for one evening as I peered, pistol in hand, from around a bush next to our house, I spotted an arrow flying straight, true, and quite fast, directly toward my left eye. I tried to duck away, but didn't make it. Fortunately, I turned enough that the arrow struck just between my eye and the bridge of my nose. The arrow bounced off, taking a small chunk of skin with it, leaving me with a bloody face and a symbol of my service in the Indian Wars of which I was kind of proud. My mother, on the other hand, was not at all impressed.

Minor Triumphs – First Dandelion of Spring

Somewhere around the first of April in perhaps the third grade, just before releasing us for the lunch recess our teacher presented us with a challenge. A contest to see who in the class could find, and return with, the first dandelion of the season.

Living nearby, I went home each day for lunch, and my normal route was the alley from the Bardwell School playground to Weston Avenue, which ran past the emergency room entrance at Copley Hospital, in its original configuration. There, on the front lawn of the first house east of the hospital, presented in its bright yellow glory against the newly green grass, was just what I was seeking – a dandelion.

I plucked the specimen and carefully nurtured it through lunch and back to the classroom where, wonder of wonders, I was the only kid in class to have done so. This led to congratulations by the teacher before a no doubt envious class, and one further "reward."

I was required to go next door with my teacher to the other third grade class and explain to them why and how I had obtained my treasure. This, at eight years old, was my first experience with public speaking, but if memory serves, pride of accomplishment overcame whatever nervousness I might have had at presenting to strangers.

So, for the rest of the day, I was the teacher's pet and drew grudging admiration from my classmates. Perhaps as soon as the next day, however, the same teacher would send me to stand, embarrassingly, in the hall for some misdeed. Fame is fleeting.

A Star Is Born, Almost

My thespian career at CM Bardwell Elementary School was brief; two performances in fact. The first – my shining moment –

occurred when I played the lead in the third (or fourth?) grade school play, the subject of which was the danger of not eating a good breakfast. The method for presenting this message was a takeoff on the currently popular TV police drama, *Dragnet*.

The opening character, Johnny, whom you would initially think to be the star, foolishly skipped breakfast. Arriving at school, he sat at his desk – at the edge of the stage – and promptly fell asleep. It was then somehow conveyed that the remainder of the story was what Johnny's dreamt, while slumped at his desk missing his lessons. That's where I came in.

In the dream, an egg, Humpty Dumpty, was spurned and fell (pushed?) from a wall, breaking into pieces. The police were notified and two detectives were assigned to solve the crime.

In keeping with the breakfast metaphor, the detectives were a slice of toast – the star, ME!! – and his partner, a pat of butter, played by my classmate, Billy Stoner. We questioned the other breakfast items, juice, potato, etc. We then reasoned and solved the mystery; Johnny had not eaten his breakfast. In due time, we faded from the scene, and Johnny, and of course the audience awoke with a greater understanding of the need for proper nutrition.

Oddly perhaps, I remember the rehearsals more than the actual performance. In particular, I recall that every time I spoke a dramatic or meaningful line, I was to pause while a teacher at the orchestra pit piano would bang out the signature five notes of the *Dragnet* theme – just like on TV. In the beginning, each time this would happen, I would look down at the piano. Through the rehearsal process, I was carefully coached to ignore the piano and to gaze at the audience until the music ended. This, I'm pleased and proud to say, I learned well, and did not slip up once.

After the regimen of rehearsing, the performance itself went off without a hitch. I comfortably and easily delivered my lines, despite wondering at the start where my parents might be. I had not seen them before the play started, and I now could not search the audience for them. But I soldiered on, and after a few minutes, I was relieved to see the silhouettes of my mother, holding my brother David, and my father in the doorway at the back of the auditorium on the way to their seats.

The play was a great success. I and the rest of the cast received rave reviews – even Johnny, who slept through the whole thing.

Alas, my next performance was in a supporting role as one of four dancing mushrooms in the following year's production of *Fantasia*. Thoroughly charming, I'm sure, but anonymous. And with that my career as an actor, and a dancer as well, was over.

The Allen Family

Of my friends at CM Bardwell Elementary School, my very best friend was Clifford Allen, son of the proprietor of a small grocery store on Marion Avenue near Fourth Street. The Allen family also resided on Marion Avenue, on the other side of Fourth Street, a couple of houses from the corner.

The Allen house had the typical backyard of the day, a modest expanse of grass, and a garage whose entrance faced the block dividing gravel alleyway. A curiosity, the Allen house had two back doors; one, on the right (as seen from the backyard), providing entrance to the kitchen, and another leading up and into the adjacent dining room. Each back door had a small concrete stoop, and between them was what I thought at the time to be the best feature of the house – a large sandbox.

Not a box in the accepted sense; this perhaps 4 foot x 10 foot sand-filled enclosure was bounded by the rear foundation of the house, the aforementioned two stoops, and a low barrier along the narrow concrete walk which joined them. In the center of the foundation there was a tap, ostensibly for the backyard hose, but which was also our water source for the pools and canals and rivers which we sometimes sculpted into the sand.

On any given day, this sandy space might be transformed into hills and valleys where troops of green plastic soldiers would fight fierce battles. On another day, toy steam shovels and dump trucks might assist in landscaping and in the construction of houses and other buildings – occasionally on a river, or sometimes lakeside – as we transformed the area into one venue or another.

Often Clifford's older brother, Gary, would play with us in the sandbox, and sometimes in the yard at various games; that is until he aged a bit and heard the siren song of other pastimes. But whether with Gary, or with some other neighborhood kids, or just my friend Clifford, I loved that sandbox.

This was all enhanced by my friend's parents, Mr. and Mrs. Allen (Claude and Alice), who were wonderful to me, and treated me as if I were family. And at Allen's Market, we were always welcome when we came in for a candy bar, or the occasional Fudgesicle.

Going for a Drive

It seems almost unimaginable these days, but for a while in the mid-1950s, my family didn't have a car. The '41 Chevy stopped running at some point, and despite the hoopla of prosperity and the expanding economy, likable Ike presided over a couple of dandy recessions. My father, despite a good, steady job as a skilled machinist, was laid-off or on strike several times during the decade, and in those days if you remembered the depression, which our parents all certainly did, you didn't just rush off to buy what you needed on easy credit terms. The bus, or often a co-worker, would take my father to work, and if my mother and I went shopping, or occasionally to the Turner Hall downtown for Friday Night Bingo, the bus was there for us, too. It was, therefore, quite an occasion when we all marched down to Louis Weeks' used car lot on Lincoln Avenue to buy the vehicle in which, several years later, I learned to drive – a gray 1950 Plymouth sedan.

Thereafter, it was a regular after dinner event to "go for a drive" in the '50 Plymouth. With Dad at the wheel, Mother riding shotgun, and me in the back seat – later joined there by my brother, David – we would motor the dead-flat landscape surrounding Aurora. I remember some landmarks; The Blackberry Creek, a meandering stream which we crossed and re-crossed as it twisted and turned, weaving its weary way through the farmlands; Deerpath Road, an aptly named country lane; and Route 30, the "Great Lincoln Highway." Starting at Times Square and terminating at an overlook at Pt. Lobos in San Francisco, it was, and remains today, in Illinois anyway, a simple two-lane thoroughfare. But knowing what it was in the larger sense allowed a small boy to feel connected, via that asphalt strip, to the entire country.

Occasionally, as we wandered, the radio would be playing

and I recall a couple of the songs from the time, which I still associate, to some extent, with our evening rides. The poignant and plaintive "See You in September" by the Tempos went on to become one of my all-time favorites, while "So Rare" by Jimmy Dorsey and His Orchestra had the opposite effect. For no known reason, whenever I heard that song, I was over-whelmed with a feeling of depression, sadness, and perhaps even a sense of dread. Very Strange.

But these jaunts usually ended on a happy note, often with a stop at the Dairy Queen for a cone, or on *very* special evenings, to the Fruit Juice House for a Malt.

Childhood:
The 1950s – The Middle Years

Thanksgiving – Part One: Morning

Though earlier and later years offered different experiences, the fondest Thanksgivings of my memory are those of my grade school years. Days which started well before dawn and seemed to just fade to a close in the not so late evening.

Those long-ago days would begin with an early morning ride with my father in the '50 Plymouth, through the still dark countryside south and east of Aurora. We would park in the barnyard of the Haag farm on Wolf Road, which seemed to me, at the time, to be a very long way from home. We would gather our stuff, and then walk a good distance past fence lines and hedgerows, past and between fields of both harvested and still standing corn. There to await the dawn when, with the coming of the light, it would be permissible to hunt for pheasant and rabbit.

We would find a suitable spot and settle in to await the sunrise. Dad would break out a thermos and there we would sit, just the two of us, alone in the half light in what seemed to me to be a wilderness, for a few precious moments, talking and sipping strong, hot, black coffee from paper cups. It tasted awful, but it was "a man's drink" and I drank it, proud to be there sharing it with my dad.

When it was full light, Dad would pack the thermos, load the shotgun, and we would set off into the corn. His interest was pheasants, and that's where they were to be found. Rabbits, on the other hand, lived along the fence lines and were almost too easy. Dad would take a rabbit or two, but would refuse to eat them unless "we had had a hard freeze," which he said was required to kill some kind of bacteria which lived within them. Later, before we left for home, we would give the rabbits to the farmer as a way of saying thanks for access to the land. The farmer would grind them up as feed for the feral cats, which helped to reduce the numbers of the other critters, unwanted residents of the barn and silos.

But it was pheasants that Dad liked to hunt, partly because they tasted so good, and partly because they were so difficult. Pheasants would hide in the corn and not fly, even if you walked closely past them. They would usually fly only if they felt threatened, or if, as I once did, you stepped on one. *Then* they would fly up – startlingly, past your face – and into the autumn wind, which bore them quickly away. But Dad was quick with the shotgun, and a good shot, so if he saw one he usually got one

I would follow along safely behind, or in a rear quarter, wearing a smaller version of Dad's hunting vest – the kind with large pouches sewn in, so I could do my part and carry a pheasant, or a couple of rabbits.

By midmorning, it was time to hike back out of the fields and unburden myself of the rabbits. We would stop at the farmhouse to say thank you and goodbye to Mr. and Mrs. Haag (Don and Bertie – family friends and distant relatives through marriage). Then it was back into the '50 Plymouth for the long drive home, where the *other* best part of the day would begin.

Thanksgiving – Part Two: The Holiday Feast

Arriving home from our Thanksgiving morning hunting trip, Dad and I would shed our heavy coats and boots in the newly enclosed back porch, and enter the house through the kitchen. We were a bit chilled, of course, from our morning in the cold November fields, and the sudden entry into a kitchen filled with the warm, wonderful smells of a Thanksgiving dinner in the making was one of life's great moments.

The aroma, and the steamed windows, created a cozy, warm, and "at home" atmosphere that is seldom matched. My mother, and Grandma, and an aunt or two, would be bustling about, seemingly doing several things at once, as preparations for the afternoon's feast progressed on schedule.

We were quickly hustled out of the kitchen – and out of the way – but not before I was given a large cup of hot chocolate to take to the living room where my uncles would be waiting, watching the Macy's Thanksgiving Day Parade from New York. Even on the "state-of-the-art" low resolution, black and white, 12-inch screen, I liked the parade – the floats, the bands, and the balloons. The crowds and the occasional street views of 6th Avenue and 34th Street, so very different from small-town, Midwestern Aurora, were fascinating to me – like every other little kid of my time.

Other than last week's Notre Dame Highlights (sponsored by The Plaster Institute), there wasn't too much football on TV in those days – especially on a Thursday, holiday or not – so my uncles and my dad chatted while they half-heartedly watched. Occasionally, one of the ladies would take a break from the kitchen and watch the parade for a few moments, with commentary on how wonderful it all looked.

The parade ended with the arrival of Santa Claus, signaling the start of the Christmas season; the parade was sponsored by a department store, after all. But Thanksgiving, and the extended autumn, weren't over just yet. After the end of the parade, and a bit of brief post-festivities commentary, there was a return to normal weekday programming. In due time, the TV was turned off, however, as it was getting to be almost time for dinner.

Our "dining room" – the not so large space between the kitchen doorway and the large archway to the living room – had been transformed. The modest table within had grown by means of something called leaves, and was now covered with a spotless white cloth. On the cloth, along with a couple of candles, were dishes, crystal, and silverware, which were only seen a couple of times a year. The men were pressed into service and began filling the strategically located empty spaces on the table with all of the traditional foods of a Thanksgiving dinner, crowned of course by a large, golden brown, wonderful smelling turkey.

Not being a toddler or an infant – as my brother and my two cousins then were – I also helped, carrying baskets of rolls and trays of olives, and the like to the table. When it came time to sit, there was no lesser "kids table." All of my "peers" had highchairs and I sat right there at the table with the grown-ups. There's not much to say about the dinner itself, other than it was wonderful. I responded to an occasional question, but I mostly didn't chat much during the meal. Although I listened closely to what was being said around the table (you can learn a lot by paying attention), I was much too busy eating to join in.

After dinner, the table was cleared, and the kitchen put in order – with but brief, lethargic, and half-hearted efforts by the men. But I was certainly volunteered to help. It was important to clean up right away, for the table would be needed again, in an hour or so, for coffee and homemade pie. The delayed coffee and dessert was every bit as good as the dinner, but by the time we were finished, things were starting to get a bit hazy for me, and the next thing I knew I was waking up the next morning in my bed, with no memory of how I got there.

As I lay there, I soon realized that 1) It was a Friday, but no school, and 2) it was now Christmas time. So I got up and had a bowl of corn flakes to fortify me as I prepared to meet the new season head-on.

The Music before Rock 'n Roll – Part One

Throughout the years of my childhood, Saturday nights were always special, whether at Aunt Goldie's or watching monster movies on *Shock Theater*, Channel 7's late-fifties Saturday night horror movie format, or just being at home with the family. While Friday night had its fights, sponsored by Gillette – "*Look Sharp, Feel Sharp, da da dat, da da*" – the more memorable Saturday night staples were the *Jackie Gleason Show*, and the old radio favorite, *Your Hit Parade*, now on TV, sponsored by Lucky Strike – "*LS/MFT.*"*

---

* Lucky Strike Means Fine Tobacco

The cast of *Your Hit Parade* would sing a musical countdown of the top seven songs of the week, *"as determined by a tally of record sales and jukebox plays."* Usually solo, but sometimes in pairs or as a group, the cast members, Dorothy Collins, the perky Doris Day-like blonde, Snookie Lanson, the all-American fraternity guy, crooner Russell Arms, and Gisele MacKenzie, the pretty, but more subdued, brunette (who was my favorite), would sing the week's selections accompanied by unnamed dancers and cast members who would occupy a scene appropriate to the song being performed.

This was my primary exposure to the popular music of the years just before rock 'n roll. And as a child, I would watch enthralled, not only by the countdown, but by the music itself. Many of those songs, including "Stranger in Paradise," "You Belong to Me," "Love Is a Many Splendored Thing," and of course, "Autumn Leaves" remain with me today as early favorites.

And though I'm thoroughly devoted to the music of my generation, and of my time, I will always remember my introduction to the music of the adult world, and the beauty of the words and the melodies of the mid-1950s will stay with me always.

The Mosquito Fogger

One intermittent and "looked forward to" summer evening event, when I was a kid, was the Mosquito Fogger. A city truck, pulling a trailer with a large tank of insecticide and the fogging device, would slowly cruise the residential streets. Powered by a small gasoline engine, which announced its presence a couple of blocks away, the fogger would generate clouds of what we thought of as smoke.

Gravitating to the sound of the engine, flocks of children would walk along behind the fogger, inside the dense cloud of "smoke," breathing in deeply the strange smelling vapor. We all thought this was great fun. The guys in the truck ignored us and parents didn't seem bothered by it all. But, despite what seems obvious today, we all seem to have survived.

Actually, I think the mosquitoes mostly survived the experience as well.

The TV Generation

We, the baby boomers, were the generation raised by, shaped by, and some said ruined by, that most powerful cultural, social, and scientific invention of all time – until the smartphone, that is. I'm speaking, of course, of the television.

TV was developed and functional by 1939, but the impending war sort of took precedence. So, the first popularly available TVs started to appear about the time I was born. Most of what was shown on early TV were simply contemporary radio programs with pictures and crude sporting events – baseball, professional wrestling, of course, and roller derby, at the time an obscure sport played in former marathon dance arenas, quickly discovered by producers as a "new" event to broadcast. And the grown-ups of the day loved it, all of it, and couldn't get enough.

By the time we "boomers" were old enough to appreciate what we were seeing, TV was an established and permanent part of daily life. And the nation *was* influenced. in society and in politics. As powerful as Roosevelt's "fireside chats" had been to an earlier generation, they didn't compare with the impact of actually seeing, live, the political heavyweights of the day. The famous Kennedy/Nixon debate was thought to be a win for Nixon by those who listened on the radio, but was a decisive victory to those many more who not only heard the words, but actually *saw* the candidates.

The pastoral baseball gave way as the nation's pass-time to the technical football at just the time when TV developed the ability to show the detail of each play, and then to show it again.

As we progressed through the fifties and "small screen" programming advanced and improved, TV shows, from *Ozzie and
Harriet*, to *The Lone Ranger*, to *Lassie* and *Lucy*, to soap operas,
and the ubiquitous police and private eye dramas, became an
important part of everyone's everyday life.

I admit I was as much enthralled with TV as anyone. However, in my freshman year of high school, I was profoundly
influenced by a single episode of a fairly run-of-the-mill
program, of which I will speak about a bit later.

The Last Day of School

During my tenure at CM Bardwell Elementary School, the
last day of each school year was special for several reasons. One,
the day was usually over by lunchtime, which was good, because
by this time we could barely stand the wait. Two, the "gym
shoes" purchased by Mom at the beginning of the previous September to be used, of course, only for gym class, were now yours
to wear (and wear out) all summer long. And three, the thing
which really made this day so special was that it was the LAST
DAY OF SCHOOL.

Until next September that is, but which – when you are 10 – is
so infinitely far into the future as to have no consequence, or
meaning when the long anticipated day of freedom had actually,
amazingly, arrived. The day was always a bit surreal; getting up
that morning was easier, the walk to school tingled with anticipation. The colors of the flowers seemed brighter and more vivid,
and the newly leaved trees fuller, and somehow greener, as the
warm, fresh, and springtime clean air softly moved them about.

Each year's last day was the culmination of a week of roller
coaster emotions. After the brief, tantalizing, "almost there"
feeling of Memorial Day weekend, restless students were pulled

back, and once again enclosed by the walls, and the regimen, of grade school as the longest week of the year began. How tedious to finish that final book report, to read that final lesson, while just beyond the glass lie a world of dreams.

This final day of the school year was different from the day before the 11 or 12 days we had off for Christmas and the New Year, or the beginning of the all too brief Easter week hiatus. On those "last" days, terrific as they were, we could see well enough into the near future to anticipate the end of the break, and know it was temporary. Before long, we would return to the same old routine.

But summer was long. And yes, we of course understood that someday, in the far future, we would have to come back. In due time, stores – where new "school clothes" and new gym shoes could be purchased – would begin to advertise "Back-to-School" sales. But that was a whole summer away, and when we did return, it would be to a different grade, to a different teacher, and to a different and hopefully better year.

Also, when we returned, we would be older. Not in time so much; the age difference between the third grader in June and the fourth grader in September was minimal. But the emotional reality – that is to say, how you *felt* – was huge. With each new grade, we would literally stand a bit taller, and walk the halls with more experience and confidence.

But all of that lay ahead, and was not considered on that special day in early June when the final bell would ring, and time ceased to exist as we donned our gym shoes and passed into a different state of being. Summer Vacation.

Saturday Night Movies

Sometime after the mid-point of the 1950s, when I was around 12 years old, there was a period of time when virtually every Saturday night my mother's sister Ersilia (Aunt Sia to me, a name I learned as a toddler and never abandoned) and her husband, Uncle Ray, would come to our house for the evening. With Grandma to babysit my cousins, John and Donald, it was, I'm sure, a welcome night out for them. They came to play cards – a curious, but currently popular game called "Rook" – and to consume a modest number of "highballs," and generally to spend the evening together gabbing around the kitchen table.

I paid little attention to the activities in the kitchen, for it left me alone in the next room with the freedom to do as I pleased (within reason), and with complete control of the television. Additionally, this being Saturday night, I did not have to go to bed.

Other than those previously mentioned, I don't recall too many of the prime time TV offerings of these particular nights, but at 10:30 pm it was always a movie. These were mostly the classic Universal Pictures horror movies, or recycled WWII era films, heavy on propaganda, with Americans valiantly holding on against the Japanese onslaught or, in late and post-war films, exacting revenge for fallen comrades in a difficult but inevitable march to victory.

Coffee and Pastries

When the Saturday night TV movie ended and the card game in the kitchen broke up, more or less simultaneously, the best part of the evening was just beginning. While the ladies tidied up and made coffee, my father, my uncle, and I set off to the B & B Bakery in North Aurora, which was just then making sweet rolls for Sunday morning. They also sold "fresh from the oven" pastries to those wise enough to come and knock on the door in the middle of the night. Returning home, we would all sit at the kitchen table and enjoy very fresh, still warm sweet rolls and coffee.

Yes, I had coffee at that age, and in the middle of the night as well. I already was an experienced coffee drinker, having learned the habit from my grandmother. When I was younger, and my parents both worked during the daytime hours, I would be dropped off to spend the day at Grandma's. I would go back to sleep, of course, and upon re-awakening at 8:30 or so, it was time for breakfast. Grandma was from the old country and her concept of breakfast was different from many others. She would provide me with the appropriate coin and send me off to Delmonico's store to purchase a round of fresh Italian bread while she made coffee.

Returning home, I would sit at the kitchen table with Grandma and enjoy Italian bread and coffee – an old country peasant breakfast she learned as a girl. My coffee was a great deal less strong than Grandma's though, and was well-laced with cream and sugar. As I learned then, I still drink coffee this way today – not too strong, with cream and sugar (well, Coffee-Mate and Splenda, but still true to principle).

Grandma's Garden

I have many great memories of the summer days I spent at my grandma's house in the heart of Aurora's "South End." One of them is of her wonderful garden. As the land sloped gently away from the back porch, a small concrete walk led from an abbreviated back lawn into and through the garden, ending beneath a trellis, covered in season by some sort of flowering vine. With neatly tended vegetables on one side, and the mad jumble of many different flowers on the other, I remain convinced that this was the perfect garden.

The bifurcated growing area seemed quite large to me as a boy, measuring perhaps 30 x 50 feet. The wild unstructured floral array was beautiful from any angle, and as the summer progressed, fresh from the vine tomatoes, and peppers, and carrots pulled from the ground – immediately washed beneath the faucet at the side of the house – provided excellent "snacks."

These were supplemented, of course, by the penny (and two for a penny) candies available at Prisco's store, provided that we could actually get our hands on a penny or two.

I can also remember Grandma standing over the flame of the gas stove burning feather remnants off of chicken necks (also acquired at Prisco's), the smell of which killed the appetite for any kind of snack. The resulting dinner, however, was as usual worth any price. Grandma was a true genius in the kitchen; a talent which, I'm pleased to attest was passed on to my mother.

Thank You, Grandma

Actually my story would not have been written at all if not for Grandma, who actually saved my life, so I'm told, when I was five years old. I was a patient at Copley Memorial Hospital, having just had my tonsils removed. This was, however, before I was compensated for the ordeal with the promised "tons of ice cream."

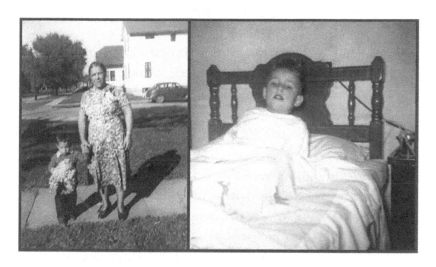

I was dozing in the child-size hospital bed, with Grandma sitting quietly in attendance, when something happened and I started to choke. As I began to turn blue, Grandma leapt into action. She immediately ran into the hall for help, becoming so excited she completely lost her English, as she ran about clutching at the staff and shouting in Italian.

Her efforts were successful; she was so energetic and insistent that she quickly received help. The blockage was cleared and all was well. Thank you, Grandma. If it never occurred to me to say it when I had the opportunity – Thank you very much. For Everything.

Many years later, I was told that two months before I came home from Viet Nam, and one month before she died, my grandma was quoted, out of the blue, as saying, "I wish I could see Tommy again." While I don't think it was ever mentioned again, I've never forgotten, and I too wish with my entire heart that I could sit in that quiet sunlit kitchen one more time, having coffee and bread with my grandma, Angelina Quagliano Desamonde.

The Music Before Rock 'n Roll: Part 2

Maybe it was my age, but when I was very young and listening to the grown-up's music, there seemed to be a wistful, almost haunting quality to many of the popular songs of the 1950s.

"(Once I Had A) Secret Love," the melancholy "September Song," and the plaintive "See You in September" (which really wasn't about September at all), the ethereal "Stranger In Paradise," and the travelogue, "You Belong to Me," all sounded to my child's ear to be quite exotic. And I liked it.

There was a song in 1955 which appealed to something in me, and which still tugs at a chord within when I hear it, "The Wayward Wind" by Gogi Grant. This falls into a category of songs which tell of such things as hearing the sound of a lonesome railroad whistle, and wanting to be going somewhere, anywhere, just to be on the move. There are many such songs, but few as spot on as Lee Marvin* singing "Wand'rin' Star" from the 1951 Broadway musical, *Paint Your Wagon*:

> *Wheels are made for rollin', mules are made to pack*
> *I've never seen a sight that didn't look better looking back,*
> *I was born under a wand'rin' star, a wand'rin' wand'rin' star"*
> *Alan Jay Lerner and Frederick Loewe 1951*

As I have said, for the most part, I liked the grown-up music of my childhood very much.

---

* (from the '69 film)
https://www.youtube.com/watch?v=El9eCRisbDo

The counterpart to all of this, it seems, was the music which accompanied the closing credits of *Sky King* on TV. On Sunday evening, when the show ended, the closing credits would roll as Sky's plane– viewed from slightly above the forward right quarter – would glide silently through the air and the closing theme music would play. And as I heard the music, a wave of sadness would wash over me. Though I'm sure not intended to be, this music was mournful, and additionally, it signaled the end of the weekend and early to bed. For Sunday was a school night, after all, the prelude to a long week of confinement in whatever grade I was trapped in at the time.

As you have no doubt realized by now, I really did not like grade school very much.

Other Places to Go, More Kids to Know

Aside from where I lived, in the area around Copley Hospital and CM Bardwell Elementary School, there were a couple of other Aurora neighborhoods in which I felt quite at home. My mother's childhood home, that is to say Grandma's house, where I spent many a summer day, was in the heart of what was then known as the "South End," Aurora's Italian neighborhood.

Also, there was a rather curious, to me at least, neighborhood known as Moecherville. This was the sort of pre-planned community to which many returning vets and their families flocked after World War II. Formerly farmland at the east edge of town, Moecherville was a crosshatch of curb-less streets and generally small houses. Many of these single-family homes were actually less than small – they were tiny. With no basement, the central heating unit, an oil furnace, held a prominent place in the living room, and if the family had two siblings who shared a bedroom, as my friend did, out of necessity they slept in bunk beds.

Although simple, even by the standards of the day, these

homes fulfilled the dreams of many young couples – children of the Depression and survivors of the war – providing them with the luxury of their own home, security, and peace, all of which, just a few years prior, existed only in their imaginations.

My Friend Bobby

A childhood friend of my mother's, Jean Hart, her husband Jerry, two sons, and at the time, a very young daughter lived in a house in Moecherville. Jerry was an Army veteran who had experiences similar to my father's. All in all, they were quite good friends of my parents. The benefit to me of all this was that their younger son Bobby was just my age, and to whom I had been introduced to shortly after we were born. Needless to say, Bobby and I were also close friends. So, I had yet another part of town which I enjoyed and where I felt comfortable, with a number of friends and acquaintances, and the opportunity to experience an altogether different neighborhood dynamic.

Ironically, as the houses were small, many of the yards were large, offering lots of room to run and play, and being when this was, the neighborhood was overrun with kids more or less my age. Moecherville was, like most neighborhoods in those days, a textbook example of the baby boom in action.

My mother visited her friend often enough, and the couples occasionally went out on Friday or Saturday nights, so I spent many days, as well as a fair number of evenings and overnights, at my friend's house, playing games and sharing Bobby's bunk bed, while his surly and disdainful older brother, Punkin' (Jerry Jr.), slept above. Looking back, Jerry Jr. may have been a pretty good guy, but as a newly minted teenager, he was far too cool be nice to his little brother – at least in front of me.

Playing "Foto-Electric Football"

Evenings at my friend Bobby's house in Moccherville were often spent playing – not often enough in my opinion as I loved playing it – an older game (introduced in 1941) called Foto-Electric Football. This wasn't the newer, similarly named, and rather stupid game featuring a miniature tin stadium which vibrated, sending 22 metal figures, one with the tiny felt football, in any and all directions.

The true Foto-Electric Football was a game where two players, Offense and Defense, selected real plays and defensive schemes which were etched into cards. These were then stacked onto a small light table. When the underlying screen was withdrawn, allowing light to shine through the play cards, the results were slowly revealed. Gains or losses were then represented on the game board, which of course looked like a gridiron, including ball position and down markers. I don't recall if I won more than I lost, or if in fact I sucked at it, but I do remember how much fun we had.

> *Author's Note: Bobby and I lost touch when we both went to Viet Nam at the same time, but to different places, with different services. In the spring of 2014 a couple of things happened more or less simultaneously. EBay provided me with the opportunity to purchase a well-preserved example of the original Foto-Electric Football, and Facebook provided the means to re-connect with my friend – which, after many years, we did.*
>
> *I was hopeful at the time for the chance to again play a game or two. But, sadly, I will not have the chance. My friend passed away later that year (from lung damage resulting from exposure to Agent Orange) and the possibility was lost forever.*
>
> *I am dedicating this passage, and the one previous, recalling my memories of Moecherville, to my dear childhood friend Bobby, or as he was known to the world at large, Robert Hart.*

My Neighborhood: Part One – The Witch

From the time I was born in 1946 to the mid-sixties, I lived on Weston Avenue on Aurora's east side, a neighborhood which was annihilated for parking by Copley Memorial Hospital. That was before it closed and moved its operations to a newer, larger, and one would suppose, better – if not more convenient – location.

This was a simple, very typical working-class neighborhood in the heartland of 1950s America, located about 45 miles west of downtown Chicago. A visit to the big city in those days required a grueling day trip along IL Route 34 (Ogden Ave) through what seemed to be a dozen small communities. This made, for my family anyway, seeing a ball game at Wrigley Field a once per summer event. Later, the newly built East-West Tollway would take us through seemingly endless cornfields, the western suburbs, and on into the city, but it would still seem to be quite the journey.

Other than the annual visit to Wrigley, and infrequent trips to Southern Illinois to see friends, we really didn't travel much. We took the '50 Plymouth twice to the Mississippi River: once to visit my father's brother in East Moline, Illinois, and once for, well, just for the drive I guess. So, for my childhood years, Aurora was pretty much the whole world, and of course, the street on which we lived was at the heart of it all. I thought, growing up, that it was a nice neighborhood, verdant green in summer with a lot of oak trees and – until the mid-fifties – no small number of elms as well. As for the neighborhood residents themselves, our street, perhaps like all streets everywhere, contained a rich diversity of characters, several of whom I will comment on in due time, starting now with:

The Witch: The house next door to ours to the west was a side-by-side duplex with a seemingly ever-changing stream of either vacancies or new neighbors whom we never really got to know.

The side of the house away from ours was occupied by its owners who, in my earlier memories, were Mr. and Mrs. G__, a curious and semi-hermitic couple who were the neighborhood oddities of my early childhood. This changed profoundly on a dramatic summer Saturday afternoon in 1953 when the Mrs. returned home to find the Mr. seated at the kitchen sink with opened wrists.

When the neighborhood excitement and novelty wore off, Mrs. G__ had become the Widow G__ who continued to live there for many years. She lived alone with seemingly no visitors. She continued to manage the duplex, and would quickly go well beyond eccentric and reclusive. Looking back, this was kind of sad I suppose, but memory suggests that she really *wasn't* a very nice person.

Inevitably perhaps, she was soon thought by the neighborhood children to be a witch, a notion which was both scary and delightfully exciting at the same time. To her advantage, I suppose, since this reputation meant that we neighborhood kids left her strictly alone – even on Halloween, no tricks – fearing to some degree, both her and whatever powers she might possess.

At roughly the time I graduated from high school, the G__ house became the first to be sacrificed for the block-and-a-half wide, and block-long – and ultimately useless – parking lot, which my old neighborhood has become. The immediate, if temporary, benefit to members of my family was that rather than being torn down, the house was put on blocks and moved. This fascinated and delighted the neighborhood kids of my brother's age, entertaining them and leaving them with an empty basement hole in which to play. But soon enough, the hole was filled as the lot became parking for the Weston Avenue Clinic. This provided extra parking for us as well, as the now gravel-covered empty lot provided space for the family car just a few feet from our kitchen door.

My Neighborhood:
Part Two – The Herald and the Family Next Door

The Herald: On the other side of the G__ house lived the E__ family – unfortunately, White Sox fans – who had a son, Robert, who was one year younger than I, with whom I often roamed the summer streets of 1950s Aurora. The E's also had another son the same age as my brother, and our parents were also friends. So it all worked out quite well.

The E__ house was also a duplex; this one, oddly, front and rear. In the early years, the E's lived in the rear unit and rented the larger front, but somewhere early in my grade school years, they made the switch and occupied the front apartment, and then of course rented the rear.

For a time, in my junior high school years, the rear portion of the duplex was occupied by the I __ family who had two older boys and a girl, April, who was my age and on whom I would have not so much a crush, but a bit of an infatuation. But like most of the temporary residents of the neighborhood, in time they moved on and that was that.

I recall, one early spring afternoon, walking past the E__ house on my way home from Bardwell Elementary School. Just as I was passing their house, Mr. E__ poked his head out the front door to inform me that my brother, who had been quite sick, had been diagnosed with pneumonia. Thus informed, I quickened my pace and hustled home to find out what I could do to help.

Some years later, I recall being informed in similar fashion that "Oswald was shot!" As the years rolled by, whatever the news of the day – local or otherwise – Mr. E__ could be counted upon to pop out and inform whoever might be passing by.

****

The Family Next Door: Moving into the somewhat larger house just to the east of ours was a couple who had children the same ages and genders as my siblings and who, after moving in, quickly became pretty good friends of my parents. Their moving in was also good for me in a couple of ways. The first benefit was that before too long I would be presented with the opportunity to make a little cash babysitting on some Saturday nights.

Also fortuitous was that the man of the house had a part-time hobby repairing television sets, and occasionally radios, in his basement. When I was in junior high and became obsessed with the workings of radios, televisions, and all manner of electronics, my neighbor took me under his wing and I spent a lot of time in his basement tinkering, and soldering, and learning. As luck would have it, he was also very good friends with a Mr. McCarville, the electricity/electronics teacher at East High. When a year or so later I advanced to that level, I had an in which allowed me extra tutelage and opportunities in the electronics lab.

The families remained great friends through the years until they both – and the E's as well – read what the hospital was writing on the wall and moved on.

The Neighborhood:Part Three – The Hoodlum & the Girl Across The Street

The Hoodlum: To the east of the house next door was a house which must've been occupied by someone but, strange to say, if I ever knew who lived there I have long since forgotten. Just on the other side of the mystery house lived an elderly woman, Mrs. T__, who, like my grandmother, had a very nice garden in her backyard which extended all the way to the alley. But I was young and didn't really know her very well, so the alley was the only place from which I could enjoy the flowers.

Coincidentally, between the garages across the alley from the garden was a wild array of many colored hollyhocks, so when walking there, perhaps on an errand to the Buy-Rite grocery store, it was – for the width of one house, at least – kind of like being in a botanical garden.

In the mid-1950s, Mrs. T's son, a vet who my father had actually known in the Army, moved in with his wife and son, who was just my age. You would think this would be a doubly good thing and the families were supposed to be (sort of) automatically close. As it turned out, my father had never really liked the man – for good reason – and the son, Billy, who joined my class at Bardwell Elementary School, was a young hoodlum in the making.

But my parents were polite, and not wanting to cause bad feelings, they were friendly with the newcomers. Fortunately, after a couple of years, the young family moved on and relative peace returned to the neighborhood.

For years, my parents cited an incident which they felt demonstrated a result of bad parenting technique. One afternoon, Billy climbed the apple tree which then grew in our backyard, and refused to come down. My father, not wanting the boy to be hurt, nor in truth, to have a boy in our apple tree at all, tried talking him down, finally telling him that he should come down from the tree because his father would be angry. To this, Billy replied: "So what? I'll just get another whippin'." Billy did eventually come down from the tree, and as it turned out, the issue was resolved in precisely the way that everyone now expected.

****

The Girl across the Street: I can't say that I was one of those young boys who hated or had no patience for girls, until one day suddenly discovering the wonder of it all. I sort of always liked them, and when I was young there was a girl who lived across the street named Stephanie who certainly liked me.

When my mother would cross the street to visit, and I, being too young to be left alone, would be taken along, Stephanie would talk to me, and sit with me, hold my hand and embarrassingly kiss me on the cheek from time to time. The two mothers both thought this was adorable behavior for seven-year-olds – and I didn't really mind as much as I pretended.

Unfortunately (perhaps), a year or so later – long before anything could develop – the family moved to New Mexico and I never saw them again.

The Neighborhood:
Part Four – The Bobby-Soxer and the Bachelor

The Bobby Soxer: After dinner, when you couldn't wander too far from home, the neighborhood kids of varying ages would gather. We would often play at some large, collective activity until, pretty much all at once, parents would appear at doorways calling the young'uns in for the night.

There was a guy who lived across the street and a few doors down, who was a couple of years older, and whom I mostly only knew in this "after dinner" context. What I remember most about him was playing football in his backyard, and the Lionel model train set up which covered most of his attic – his father's hobby, I would guess. But he would sometimes have some of us over and run the trains himself. Neat!!

And I also remember his sister. She was older yet; a teenager, in fact. Memory suggests that she wasn't extraordinarily pretty, and I didn't have a crush on her or any such thing. In fact, I don't even remember her name. But she was different, and a somewhat notable figure in my pre-adolescent life. She clearly wasn't a grown-up, but she wasn't one of us kids, either. As such she and her friends represented a tantalizing glimpse into a world which lie just a few years away.

A world which was just then introducing a new kind of music, rock 'n roll, which was slowly creeping into the music charts, and which, it seemed only young people liked. A world where boys sometimes had cars which were different from Dad's '50 Plymouth sedan, referred to as jalopies or hotrods. Guys who were football stars at the local high school, and wore white sweaters with stripes, and numerals, and a large red "A" sewn onto the front. Boys who, whether driving their jalopy, or just walking along the street, seemed to be always with a pretty girl.

And the girls, sometimes haughty or imperious, would walk with them or with each other wearing – in contradictory fashion – either long skirts or short shorts, and of course loafers and bobby-sox.

In short, the world of the mid-fifties teenager. I was fascinated by these people who, in retrospect, were really just kids a few years older. But in the course of one's life those are critical years, and I couldn't wait to grow up a bit and join them.

****

The Bachelor: Beyond the E__ house to the west was a bit nicer than average dwelling owned and occupied by the widow, Mrs. R__. She was friendly enough, but a bit haughty and aloof to the neighborhood kids. Living with Mrs. R__ was her bachelor son, Lawrence, who was probably a bit over 30 years old at the time and, looking back, I believe was somewhat dominated by his mother. Kids of the neighborhood, while indifferent to the elderly woman, didn't like Lawrence all that much. A sentiment which I shared.

Walking with my mother one day on a shopping trip downtown, we encountered Lawrence strolling along Broadway. My mother, ever polite, stopped for a moment to say hello. But Lawrence seemed more interested in me, squatting down and speaking in such an obsequious voice that I soon found myself standing behind my mother, feeling uncharacteristically quite uncomfortable. I'm guessing that my mother understood what was happening for she quickly made excuses and hustled us away.

Had I been older, or more aware of such things, I might've expected him at some point to offer me candy, or jellybeans, or wax lips, or whatever to come inside for a while when his mother wasn't home. He didn't, and in fact never got the chance. With the sometimes unconscious wisdom of children I, like the rest of the kids on our street, walked sort of carefully around the R__ house.

The Last Out of the Game

I will, in time, elaborate on the fact that I was never really very successful at team sports. But when I was in the fourth or fifth grade, I was in a softball league, perhaps organized by the local Cub Scout troops, where I did reasonably well – with one notable exception. There was a summer evening game at Beaupre Elementary School, played on the school's small dusty diamond on the corner of Ohio Street and Galena Boulevard. I was sort of familiar with the area. Sometimes, on my family's after dinner drives, we would stop for a cone at the Dairy Queen, right across the street from the field.

Games in this league were fairly typical for 9- or 10-year-olds. Some kids rode from Bardwell School with the coach to the "away" game. Some, like myself on this evening, were driven by their parents. Parents sometimes, but not always, showed up to watch the games, and were not, in any case, the fanatical fans that parents seem to have become in more recent years.

As a team, we had no fixed positions, and in the games, players would rotate, so that in the course of a game everyone played everywhere. A notable feature of our games, however, was (again, unlike modern times), we kept score. And the score *mattered*.

Toward the end of this particular game, with one inning to go and the visiting team, us, holding the lead, it was my turn to rotate to pitcher. I assumed the mound with some confidence – we had a big lead, after all – and I got the first two guys out fairly easily. One out to go. The next batter got a hit, and with him standing on first base, something happened.

From that moment on, I could absolutely *not* get the ball over the plate. I walked the next batter on four pitches. That's okay, I thought, we had the lead and needed only one out to win the game. I walked the next batter on four pitches. It became a procession, as each time I threw the ball four times – in the general direction of home plate – the batter and runners would trot to the next base. I could see pity in the umpire's eyes, and the relish with which each new batter confidently strode to the plate, as the runs began to score. The longer this went on, of course, the worse I got.

But I kept trying. We still needed just one out to win the game. And so, while this vital fact *still* remained true, another, previously unplanned, rotation took place and I was shifted to third base. A teammate took over on the mound and I was relieved in more ways than one. And wouldn't you know it, the very next pitch resulted in a pop-up to the left side of the infield – which I camped under and deftly caught. And the game was won.

After the home team sullenly walked off the field, and our equipment was neatly packed in the coach's station wagon, we retired to the Dairy Queen across the street, where my teammates indicated that all was forgiven as they complimented me on my game-winning put-out. Funny how things work out sometimes.

Another curiosity – perhaps. For the rest of the season, I somehow never again rotated to the pitching position.

The Carpenter's Ghost

When my father was a boy, that is to say around 1920, it was not uncommon for a skilled carpenter, if he had the resources, to purchase a plot of land and build a house. He would then sell the house and use part of the proceeds to build another, and so on. When my father was young, he lived, for a time, in such a house. Years later, if our evening drive returned us to Aurora from the north and east, we would sometimes pass that house on Farnsworth Avenue, just north of New York Street. And as we went by, he would usually point or acknowledge the house in some way. The first time this happened, he told my mother and me – and David, although at his age then I'm sure he couldn't have cared less – the story of the carpenter's ghost.

My paternal grandmother was a widow with many children, of whom my father was the youngest. With no skills other than to work as a "domestic" – read "servant girl" – she was occasionally unsuccessful in keeping her family together. My father lived occasionally with an aunt, and once, briefly, in an orphanage. But my grandmother was strong-willed, and whenever possible, she would gather her brood – the younger ones at least – and live as a family.

On one such occasion a job brought her to Aurora where she found an inexpensive house to which to bring her children. Aside from being an entire house for her and her many children to live in, it had the additional benefit of being inexpensive. The reason for this was that a portion of the second floor was unfinished, the carpenter having died before completion. To my grandmother, this inconvenience was no match for the ability to live with her family in their own home, and I'm sure the kids didn't mind at all.

So they settled in and happily made do with what they had. Soon after, however, things started to "go bump in the night." Actually, sometime after midnight on many occasions, the sounds of hammering and sawing and the general clatter of carpentry could be heard coming from the unfinished, sealed-off rooms on the upper floor. The consensus was, of course, that the carpenter was returning to complete the construction of his house. This was too much for my grandmother. She soon found another place for her and her family to live, perhaps not as good, but with no uninvited workmen.

But they remained in Aurora, where some years later my father met my mother, and not too long after that, as soon as that pesky war was taken care of, my saga began. It's easy to think that my father was teasing his young family with a spooky story. But in all the years of his life, he never wavered, and always, without drama, acknowledged the house whenever we passed. Having heard him tell the story, I remain convinced that his experience was real.

Scouting: Part One – Cub Scouts

After the grueling climb up the Cub Scout hierarchy – Wolf, Bear, and the never fully understood status of Webelos – the transition to being a Boy Scout was major. I'd reached the big time, well on the way to being grown-up. Or so it seemed at the moment.

The girls had long since graduated from Brownies to Girl Scouts, a fact which caused us boys to be both resentful and a bit jealous. Of course, what we didn't know at the time was that girls *do*, in fact, mature sooner. At around age seven or eight, they begin to have deep thoughts – having a wedding to start planning, a life to organize, and Elvis, or Frankie Avalon, or Paul McCartney to fantasize about. We boys, on the other hand, would mostly remain boys to some degree for the next 15 or 20 years, occasionally longer. In the order of things important to boys/men, deep thoughts can often consist of who the Bears are playing next Sunday. But I digress.

The overtly paramilitary nature of Cub Scouting, and later Boy Scouting, was lost on us as many of the organized aspects of our lives tended, in those days, to socialize us in preparation for the conformity of the military experience.

Also, remember that we, the charter member baby boomers, grew up in the immediate aftermath of WWII, which we acted out in our play on a regular basis. So, the uniforms and regimentation, disciplines, and codes of honor, were not necessarily outside the mainstream of daily life.

The less than patient waiting to get older notwithstanding, Cub Scouts was fun. The weekly den meetings at someone's house usually provided something interesting in the area of arts and/or crafts – and yes, helped us to learn about working as a team. The den mothers worked hard at organizing stuff for us to do, and I recall quite vividly, one meeting which focused on knights and castles of the Middle Ages. We each made a shield of cardboard and painted it with a brightly colored crest. It was this single event, I believe, which sparked the interest in Medieval times which is still in me; the Teutonic Knights, King Arthur and his Round Table, The White Queen, and The Black Prince, and so on.

The monthly gathering of the entire pack, in the Bardwell School Gymnasium, complete with uniforms, ceremony, occasional awards and promotions – and a potluck supper supplied by our moms – was a looked forward to event. There was a theme to each meeting, as I recall, and although there wasn't then a President's Day in February, we did combine and celebrate the birthdays of Abraham Lincoln and George Washington as a single event. One year, before the February monthly meeting got started, I was assigned, along with some other Cubs, to attach maraschino cherries to branches, creating small cherry trees which served as centerpieces for the tables of the supper, thus honoring our first president.

But, despite all the fun, Cub Scouts was just a warm-up for the main event. Despite how slowly time seemed to grind forward, it *did* pass, and soon enough, we become Boy Scouts, eligible for even grander adventures.

Scouting: Part Two – Camp Blackhawk

As Boy Scouts, our circle of activities widened. We still had regular meetings and gatherings, of course, but we did other stuff, too; like a day in the woods identifying various shrubs (like poison ivy) and trees, and such, as well as learning to build a fire, and what knots were useful and how to tie them.

There were extended adventures as well. One fine, if more than a bit rainy, summer weekend, we camped with several other Scout troops along the Fox River at Pottawatomie Park in St. Charles, Illinois.

I also spent about 10 days at a place called Camp Blackhawk, which I heard once was somewhere in Michigan (Muskegon County, I learned much later. I knew at the time it seemed an awfully long way from home). We did the usual things; ate our meals in the communal mess hall, swam and rowed boats on the rather nice lake, and slept in semi-permanent tent structures, which held bunks for about 10 boys each.

The camp counselors were guys a few years older than we were, and each an "expert" at one of the various activities in which we participated. The counselors stayed in cabins scattered about the lakeside woods near the venues they supervised; woodcraft, archery, boating, and the like – even a small rifle range. The cabins in which the counselors stayed all had names, usually puns on the names of movies popular at the time (i.e., "Paintin' Place").

On the first day, while taking our initial tour, the rifle range caught my attention. When we were introduced to the counselor overseeing the range, he asked the group if anyone was interested in competing with him – best score for five shots with a .22 rifle.

The bet was a quarter and he would supply the ammunition (which probably meant that it was the camp's ammo).

No one stepped forward, except finally one. Me. A quarter was a fair portion of the money with which I had been supplied – with the stern instruction to spend it wisely – and the rest of the guys all eagerly told me what a fool I was, and that I couldn't possibly win. But I went forward anyway.

So down I went to the shooting counter, and we took turns firing at the target. When 10 shots were expended we walked to the paper targets to learn the results. I discovered that (surprise!) I had lost – and badly. Actually, my shots weren't that bad, but he was an ace.

I handed over my quarter and received a large number of "I told you so's" from my new friends. But that was okay; I got to shoot five rounds and be the center of attention for 15 minutes or so. And it only cost me a quarter. I still believe it was money well spent.

The days passed and we cycled through the various activities by day, rowed boats and had water fights after dinner, and generally had lots of fun. And I learned a few things as well, including the theretofore unknown joy of apple butter on breakfast toast. Surprisingly, I won an award on the archery range; an activity in which I had little real interest. I accepted the award proudly nonetheless and still have it.

On the last day, we packed up our stuff and were off on the long bus ride back to Aurora, happy to be going home, but sad to be leaving. A sign, I guess, that we'd had a pretty good time.

Scouting: Part Three – Winters at Camp Kedeka

Camping was, of course, a big feature of Boy Scouting, which was perfectly logical and expected, given the origins, nature, and mission of Scouting. We had several weekend campouts in various parks and other places. But there were other things, too. There were "merit badges" to be earned, and meetings to attend at which merit badge work could be reviewed and camping trips discussed and planned. I'm sure there was more, but that's what I remember.

The meetings, once begun, were okay. They were a bit more regimented than the Cub Scout gatherings, and for better or worse, included very little involvement by our moms. But we were older, and could go off and participate in such things by ourselves. I also, with some fondness, recall the wild, impromptu, undisciplined, "capture the flag" sort of games we would play, and which nicely counter-pointed the organized meeting that followed.

But it was the outings, in my mind at least, which seemed to be the predominant activity. As I indicated earlier, we had various campout experiences. But far and away, the ones I remember most fondly took place in winter.

Each year, deep in the winter, we would spend a couple of weekends (Friday evening through Sunday afternoon) occupying the small, rustic cabins at Camp Kedeka, in the heart of Bliss Woods in Sugar Grove, Illinois.

For a Boy Scout camp, the name Kedeka seems a nicely appropriate Indian-sounding name, but was, in fact, the concatenation of the first letters of the three counties which it served; Kendall, DeKalb, and Kane. We had no idea where we were, and could not have found Sugar Grove on a map to save ourselves, and Bliss Woods had a *much* more primitive and remote feeling than Camp Blackhawk. But the car rides to and from were much shorter, so we knew we weren't too far from home.

We would settle in late on Friday afternoon and because, as I have said, this was the dead of winter, it was already getting dark by the time we arrived. The cabins in which we stayed were actually a bit more than rustic – they were primitive.

Memory fails me here, but I'm guessing that they were each no more than 15 x 20 feet. The central feature was a large fireplace opposite the entrance. The accommodations were four wood-frame double bunks, two against each side wall. The bunks were man-size, however, so there was plenty of room, and with a thin mattress to supplement our sleeping bags, they were downright luxurious compared to sleeping in a tent on the ground, even dry ground.

Settling in, we would cook and eat our dinner, then tidy up and all gather around the fireplace of one of the cabins for stories. We were too keyed up from just being there to turn in early on Friday night, so we would sit well into the night, mesmerized by the fire, lost in the stories the troop leaders would tell which, of course, would include the terrors possibly lurking in the dark, snowy woods just outside the thin cabin door.

Saturdays were filled with activities, woodcraft and knots, of course, and usually a hike in the dense woods. We would stop for lunch at some small clearing, or beside a stream, and the troop leaders would again provide proof that a cooking fire could indeed be built and lit in the damp cold woods. After the meal, we were taught how to properly douse our fire and disperse the remnants, so as to leave the woods as we had found it.

After Saturday night's supper, and a few more stories, or sing-alongs, or whatever, we would turn in, being pretty tired on this night from the exertions of the day. This was what I was waiting for. Every time we went winter camping at Camp Kedeka, I took with me the same plan.

My intention was to sleep for a few hours, and then get up about 1 am and go for a hike on my own. I wanted very much to hike the winter woods in the complete and silent solitude of the cold, dark, snowy night. It just seemed like *such* an adventure, and I would look forward to and plan my trek for days before we would make camp.

Alas, it turned out that each time I had the opportunity I was just as tired as everyone else, and I would sleep through the night. Each time this happened I always had a tiny sense of failure. I hadn't brought my plan to fruition.

The upside was that when morning came I always awoke fresh and properly prepared for the Sunday breakfast of pancakes and sausage, which set us up nicely for Sunday's fun. I regretted missing the opportunity to have my solo adventure. But okay, I'd do it next time, for sure.

December 1st

Aside from being my father's birthday, the first day of December was a transitional moment in the cycle of each year. Thanksgiving and, sadly, the extended autumn have come to an end. But okay, the page turns and in earlier and more rational times, the Christmas season could now begin.

Christmas time arrived sort of slowly in the days of my youth. But once it was December, it was now okay for snow to fall, for we all wanted a white Christmas, and the possibility at least of experiencing an old-fashioned Currier and Ives-like scene as the season came to its fruition. Cold weather was okay, too, for if the Phillips Park lagoon was to freeze for skating, the temperature had to dip below zero for two or three nights, which in those days it almost always did in December's first couple of weeks.

As the Christmas season itself began to get rolling, spaces around the entrances of grocery stores and other shops were festooned with green pine cuttings and wreaths, and the scent of the pine perfumed the cold, often snowy, air. Bunches of mistletoe were available for hanging, and boughs of holly for hall decking.

In the background, bells could be heard as people hustled

about from shop to shop, to the market, to the lunch counter at a convenient drug store for a BLT, and finally, laden with packages, to home again. Empty lots were filled with cut fir or spruce waiting to be selected, taken home, and transformed into that most magical icon of the season, the Christmas tree, which would then dominate the living room for the next three weeks or so.

I recall the occasionally secretive nature of my mother as she acquired, and carefully hid, presents for the big day. Although I knew her hiding spots, I never peeked. Yes, the waiting was agonizing, but to know ahead of time would diminish the unmatchable special-ness of Christmas morning.

Our after dinner drives in the '50 Plymouth would take us, more than once, to join the slow line of cars navigating Lehnertz Avenue at the edge of Aurora. Homeowners of this semi-suburban street, with a lot of open land, had collectively decided to tell the story of the journey to Bethlehem and the Nativity with large cutout figures, and signs relating passages from the biblical story, and of course, many, many, many lights. Cars, laden with mothers and fathers, and of course, the children of the baby boom, came from miles around to join the parade, pausing at house after house to read the passages and admire the artwork and gaze in wonder at the lights.

At school, our classroom was transformed by our own efforts into a wonderland of colorful cut paper chains and bows, and drawings of bells and candles and holly, and all manner of Christmas decorations which we ourselves produced in – what at least seemed like – extended art periods. Absolutely the best time of the year, at least as far as school was concerned.

I recall little page-size Advent Calendars, with a small flap on the back so they could be stood up on the living room end table like a picture frame. On the front of these calendars was a painted Christmas scene of some sort, which seemed almost three-dimensional with flocked snow and silvery glitter. Little numbered doors, marking December's days, were cut into the top layer and could be opened – one per day – to reveal a Christmas message printed on the layer below. Each day, I would come home from school to open that day's door to read the underlying message, and to feel my excitement grow, knowing I was one day closer to the two-day event that was Christmas.*

---

* See the earlier chapter, "Ghosts of Christmas Past."

Junior High School – Late Fifties, Early Rock 'n Roll

1958 – 1st Year at Waldo Junior High School

Having met and surmounted the challenges of kindergarten, and endured the long, slow drag through grade school, in the fall of 1958 I achieved my next major milestone in life – The transition to junior high school. This evolution from childhood to early adolescence was characterized first by a much longer walk to and from school. Then, the melding of students from all of the grade schools on the east side (of Aurora), which led, of course, to new friends and expanding horizons, and although the "homeroom" group stayed together through the day, we had the new experience of moving from room to room, with a different teacher for each subject.

For my first year at KD Waldo Junior High School, our homeroom was the gymnasium, and our homeroom teacher, Mr. Ridell was, in fact, a PE teacher. His classroom, for homeroom anyway, was the bleachers at the far-right side corner of the gym, near the boy's locker room. After homeroom, when classes began, we would move as a group to various locations around the building, but it was to this unusual "room" that we would muster each day.

There is little to be said about this other than the fact that Mr. Ridell was something of a disciplinarian, and his method for keeping order was his old college fraternity paddle. If anyone misbehaved in homeroom, they were ordered to the foot of the bleachers, and there to bend forward from the waist. It was then that a single swat was administered; and a good solid swat it was. It usually took but one occurrence to enforce Mr. Ridell's rules of homeroom conduct. I know that's all it took for me.

The Red & Black Spot

Our first day indoctrination into my new junior high environment at Waldo was a meeting in the school's auditorium of the entire seventh grade class. The lecture included a reference to a place across the street called the "Red and Black Spot" (the name coming from the East High School colors – red and black).

What was now KD Waldo Jr High School had been, until just a year or two prior, East Aurora High School, and the Red and Black Spot was a traditional after-school hangout, complete with tables, booths, and a juke box filled with the current musical innovation, rock 'n roll. When the new high school was built, and the older kids moved away, the dynamic of the neighborhood changed. The place was not considered to be an appropriate venue for 12- and 13-year-olds, and did not survive for long.

It was still there, however, when I arrived in the fall of 1958. Many of my new classmates had older siblings who had very much liked the place, so the question was raised, and the official answer was simply to *stay away . . .* Being a (mostly) obedient lad, I can state that I never set foot in the establishment, so I can say no more about it.

Generations

Thinking back to the "Red and Black Spot" makes me realize that I just missed much of what is nostalgically recalled as the 1950s. By this, most people mean the late-fifties, much as saying the 1960s usually means the later, more turbulent part of that decade.

The 1950s usually conjures images of poodle skirts, jalopies, sock hops, Connie Francis, Brenda Lee, Frankie Avalon, and the early Elvis. Saying that I missed this is not strictly true – I was there and I experienced a lot of it, but I was too young to truly be a part of, and to fully grasp the era. We are defined, to a large degree I think, by the music of a narrow band of years – the music heard, in my case, not so much from the old Philco radio, but on my phonograph, and from an AM radio in the dashboard of a car (heard sometimes from the back seat).

A slightly older friend recounted to me, some years ago, that he was devastated when Elvis died, but felt no such emotion at the murder of John Lennon. My experience was precisely the opposite. While I was somewhat indifferent to the passage of the older Elvis, that December day in 1980 was, for me, truly "The Day the Music Died." Though separated from the cool cats of the fifties by a very few years, our generation, the baby boomers, is defined not so much by "Love Me Tender", but by "Love Me Do."

To carry the thought a bit further, I care not at all for the grunts and growls of Bruce Springsteen, while friends, just a few years younger, think he's terrific.

The Radio Kit

Early in my junior high years, I purchased, or more likely my mother purchased for me, a build-it-yourself kit marketed by the Cub Scouts. This crystal radio set was a simple device for a young lad to build. It was fairly easy; the components were all mounted to the back of a plastic panel and the most difficult part was winding copper wire around a wooden core, thus creating a tuning coil. It required an antenna, and fortunately, my bedroom window looked out upon the roof of our rear porch. So, under my father's supervision, I went out onto the porch roof to attach wooden braces to the house, and to string the antenna cable between them. An antenna lead was then routed through the window and connected to my radio. I was in business.

Not only did I successfully complete the project, I understood it. The miracle of the radio receiver was not in its construction, but in how and why it worked. I don't recall, but within the instructions, I think there must have been some explanation as to the function of each of the components. I was fascinated by that function – the flow of electrons, the synchronicity, and the concept that the completed, working device was much greater than the sum of its parts. I remember explaining, perhaps at the family Christmas gathering, to a probably very bored Uncle Ray, precisely how a radio worked, and what each of the components did, and why they did it, and the absolute wonder of it all!

My radio did not have speakers, but had instead a hand-held ear piece, not unlike the receiver of very early telephones. I would lay in bed late at night with that ear piece pressed to my ear, listening to whoever was talking on the radio. I have no idea what band I was listening to. I'm pretty sure it wasn't AM because I wasn't receiving the same programming as could be heard on the giant Philco set downstairs. One of the programs I came across was dedicated to ham radio. Apparently, some guy in a studio received transmissions from ham radio operators and the conversation was rebroadcast to me, and to whomever else was listening on that band.

In retrospect, this was very much like today's talk radio, but the topics had to do with ham radio, and the many technical issues involved. After that, I wanted nothing more than to be a ham radio operator and talk to the world. I would buy magazines dedicated to the activity. I would read the articles and the advertising, and dream of this or that piece of equipment in the way that, a few years later, I would dream of hotrods and Corvettes and Ferraris.

When I entered high school, I took classes in electricity, and soon, electronics. As I mentioned earlier (see "The Family Next Door"), our next-door neighbor repaired televisions in his spare time and happened to be pals with the high school electricity/

electronics teacher, Mr. McCarville. This afforded me opportunities and extra tutelage in a subject I was absolutely passionate about, and which I otherwise would not have been entitled.

This was all for naught, however, when sometime in my junior year, I lost interest in electronics, almost literally overnight. All of what I knew beyond the basics, I have forgotten. This experience led me to the first of several, of what I believe to be, universal truths. Nothing lasts forever.

Picnics at Fabyan Forest Preserve

I have always loved the autumn of the year. Having a birthday in early October helps a lot, but some of my fondest memories of autumn are of picnics at Fabyan Forest Preserve, which straddles the Fox River just north of Batavia, Illinois. It's more popular now and more widely used, but I'll always remember it as the simple woods it was in the second half of the 1950s. In particular, the more remote portion on the east side of Route 25.

It was here that the forest portion of Forest Preserve was more literally true. And it was here that the family – the Shropshires, the Drakes, Grandma, and Aunt Mary – would sometimes go for weekday, after work/school picnics. The family routinely gathered, of course; not just for Christmas, but for birthdays, and seemingly any excuse for a summertime cookout. But these outings were special. Not only were they weekday events in a remote location, but they only happened in the autumn, late September and October.

Turning from Route 25 onto a small gravel road led to a clearing in the woods which offered a few simple amenities, including several widely scattered picnic tables, most with a small nearby stone structure topped with a metal grate in which a cooking fire could be built. Backed into the edge of the trees, some distance away, was a woodpile containing mostly fallen limbs and such, chopped and left by the park rangers. We, the kids, were assigned the chore of gathering wood for the fire. This meant a walk through ankle deep, crispy, fallen leaves, an activity that I've always loved.

The actual gathering of wood was another matter, however, for the woodpile was infested with daddy long-leg spiders. This made wood gathering less of a chore, and more of an adventure, and was probably the first time I heard from an adult, *"They're more afraid of you than you are of them."* Reassuring as this may have seemed, I'm not quite sure it was true, as I was quite afraid of the creatures, while they merely took it as an opportunity to crawl up my arm. Eek!

But we managed to complete the mission. The fire was built and a wonderful dinner was prepared. What is commonly thought of as summertime picnic food, hot dogs, baked beans, and the like, with coffee or hot chocolate substituted for pop (soda, to some), it was perfect; hot and comforting in the crisp autumn air. And as we ate, the air glowed with the combined colors of autumn leaves and the rays from the setting sun.

As the sun set further, and the air cooled even more, dinner was finished. The area was tidied, and by the time headlights were required, we would all be in our cars heading out of the park for home.

Jennings Terrace and Hicksatomic

An event of some significance occurred in Aurora on Friday, March 13, 1959. A large plot of land between LaSalle Street and Broadway and bounded by North Avenue was the location of Jennings Terrace. Officially a "Chartered nonprofit home for elderly persons," the facility was commonly referred to as the "old folks' home." The large, old-fashioned, very institutional-looking building was completed in 1856. A five-story stone structure, sans the original attic and high steeply sloping roof, it was consumed in spectacular fashion by fire on that fateful Friday the 13th.

Waldo Jr. High was located on higher ground than was Jennings Terrace, and not too far away, so I got a pretty good view of the smoke and activity, including a couple of buzzing helicopters, from the large upper floor window of the principle's anteroom, where I was spending the afternoon, having done *something* (?) wrong.

Aside from the tragedy of the fire (four elderly residents perished in the blaze), what I remember most about the intersection of Broadway and North Avenue was the new gas station across the street. In those days, this was called a filling station, or more properly, a service station (for reasons obvious at the time, and rather less so today).

In those now forgotten times, an attendant would rush to your car, clean your windows, check the oil (in hopes of selling you a quart), check and adjust tire pressure all around, and oh, by the way, pump you a dollar or two of gasoline.

The service station on the southeast corner of North and Broadway was part of the Hick's Oil Company chain of discount gas stations, the only one in Aurora, and which was identified to the world by its new name, announced in large neon letters, "HICKSATOMIC." In the 1950s, any reference to atomic, and by extension, atomic bomb meant power. So I'm sure the name was deemed enticing as a source of fuel.

The advertising notion was defeated to some degree, however, because most of the time, so it seemed, the central letters of the sign didn't light up, and so the place was generally referred to as what the sign actually read. On those evening rides, if we were in the right part of town – perhaps heading for the Broadway Fruit Juice House for the rare but always hoped for malt – if we needed gas, we might stop at "HICK MIC."

Mrs. Rodin (Rodan)

But back to the junior high school experience. In the late 1950s, Japanese monster movies were very much in vogue. Godzilla (giant lizard), Mothra (giant moth), and Rodan (giant *flying* lizard) were repeatedly destroying Tokyo, to the horror of the citizens, and the great frustration of the Japanese military.

By coincidence, my seventh grade art teacher at Waldo was the elderly (or so, at 12 years old, we thought) Mrs. Rodin. She was immediately dubbed "Rodan," of course, and to this day, I cannot think of that art class without envisioning the giant pterodactyl.

The unflattering sobriquet notwithstanding, I really can't recall if she was a very good art teacher. I say this perhaps unfairly, but I do feel that had she been a greater influence, at least to me, as an art teacher I would probably remember more than just her name.

Ice Skating: Part 1

One Friday evening during the winter of '58–'59, while going for the customary after dinner drive, we passed through Phillips Park and I insisted that we stop so I could walk down to the city's principal ice skating rink. I had recently determined the need to learn to ice skate, but with no anticipation of how important this activity would become throughout my junior high and high school years.

The large, flooded, and frozen space, known as the lagoon, on which throngs of teenagers and others skated, was a former marsh; the low point of a bowl created in the 1930s when the Works Progress Administration (WPA) reorganized and expanded the park by digging a lake, draining marshland, and adding contour to what was theretofore a primitive, and probably pristine, wetland.

This sunken, tree-ringed patch of land was huge by skating rink standards, the oval measuring over 100 x 75 yards, and in summer, accommodated several softball diamonds. Aside from its dimensions, a key feature of the Phillips Park skating rink was the warming house located at the end of the oval closest to the park's circular drive. The "hothouse," as we called it, contained benches on which to change footwear, and to flirt with and/or otherwise bother the girls, a concession stand (popcorn, hot chocolate, pop, and candy), and a pot-bellied stove, replete with the unmistakable odors of burning coal, and scorched, wet wool.

So, on this particular winter Friday night, Dad parked the '50 Plymouth on the circle drive and I was allowed to go down to the lagoon. Whether my parents sat in the car, or followed at a discreet distance, I'll never know, but as I ran down the hill and emerged from the trees, I was confronted by a scene of absolute wonder. Illuminated by the ring of lights, which on warmer nights shone down on softball games, the vast, brightly lit expanse of ice, and the multitudes of older kids and grown-ups flashing by, convinced me that this was how I wanted to spend my winter evenings and weekends.

As luck would have it, on patrol at the spot where I had emerged was a policeman, unlucky enough to have drawn the assignment of walking around outside on a cold winter's night, and watching others have fun as he kept the peace. Not that there was a lot of peacekeeping to do. So, he was no doubt cold and bored, and I'm sure, quite amused as I breathlessly explained to him my plans to learn to ice skate, and as I "practiced" by carefully running across the ice and sliding to a stop. But he was friendly and offered encouragement, and I liked him for that. Still do, in fact, whoever and wherever he is.

Ice Skating: Part 2 –
Uncle Ray's Old Hockey Skates

The first step in the process of learning to ice skate was to actually acquire a pair of ice skates. Money was tight, as it usually was, so this was a bigger problem than it might seem. However, family conversation revealed that Uncle Ray, who was quite the athlete in his younger days, had a perfectly serviceable pair of old hockey skates, which he no longer used, and as luck would have it, were just my size.

I don't remember how I got to the park on my first outings – subsequent trips to the lagoon involved a walk of two long blocks from home to the bus stop on Fifth Avenue, a tedious bus ride, then another walk over hill and dale, through Phillips Park to the hothouse – but I probably got a ride the first time or so, until I learned the way.

Strangely, I have no memory of the learning process. My first, and subsequent, recollections of ice skating involve not only knowing how, but being pretty good at it as well. Soon I would long for a pair of racing skates, with extended blades and no restrictive ankle support. But I'll save that for another time.

Mr. Ireland's Homeroom

In September of 1959 we returned for a second year at K.D. Waldo (eighth grade). We were big shots now, and confident – not the timid newcomers of just a year ago. On the first day, we found that we had been reassigned to a different homeroom, this one supervised by a Mr. Ireland, the senior art teacher. His room, our new homeroom, was a very large upper-floor space with long, wide tables, and chairs befitting a junior high art class. Actually, as I would discover later, as an art room, this space was much better suited than those at the new high school.

Located on the third floor front of the northern "wing" of the old building, it featured very large windows on two sides, plenty of space, plus the best homeroom AND art teacher I ever had.

Science Class

There are three things that I remember about eighth grade science class. One, the class was on the top floor of the building, and as we were all filing into the classroom, before we had to take our seats, you could stand at the large, eastward-facing windows which offered great views of the rooftops, and in the fall, brightly colored trees for a very great distance. Another is that every time I think of that class, for no reason that I can imagine, I think of the song, "Way Down Yonder in New Orleans" by Freddy Cannon.

Lastly, I remember a test we were given in the middle of the fall semester. The test asked, among other things, the percentages of the gases which make up the Earth's atmosphere. I've said it before, I was not a terribly good student, but somehow I learned and remembered the composition of the Earth's atmosphere, expressed as a mix of the various gases (20% oxygen, 79% nitrogen, and 1% a bunch of other stuff), and some other materials that we had covered in class. I was somewhat surprised that I knew these answers; reading a book as homework was a chore with which I didn't often burden myself.

I don't recall the teacher's name, but he was about 30, and looked to be the kind of guy who would knock your block off if you gave him a hard time, and we were all just a bit intimidated by him, I think. The next day, he returned the graded tests to us, one by one. When he got to me, he laid the paper face down on my desk, and with a stern look, asked if I had studied for the test. Altogether intimidated now, I meekly answered, "Yes, a little."

At that, he merely repeated my words and moved on. When I turned my paper over, I discovered a large red "A" and the words, "Nice Job." That moment, like Freddy Cannon I guess, is something I will never forget.

Christmas 1959

There are moments in the flow of our lives, fixed in memory, which don't fade with the passage of time and are easily, and fondly, recalled. One of these, for me, is the Christmas season of 1959.

There was the family Christmas, of course, which was always special in itself. And I was now, at every opportunity, exercising my newly acquired ability to ice skate – my Uncle Ray's old hockey skates were serving me quite well. But those are both somewhat generic. My best memories of that time recall the after school sessions in Mr. Ireland's homeroom.

I believe Mr. Ireland felt a responsibility to his young charges that went beyond simply administering each morning's brief homeroom gathering. In the first semester of eighth grade, at 13 years old we were all – outside the comfortable circle of family and close friends – sort of feeling our way into life, awkward and shy with girls, and I truly think Mr. Ireland's mission was to help us, in his small way, to get through all of that. *(The girls, I would later come to find out, were shy and insecure as well, although we boys sure didn't know it at the time.)*

So, as the Christmas season approached, some of us, in response to Mr. Ireland's invitation to the homeroom class, started spending a few afternoons after classes were over helping to create Christmas decorations. Not just for our room, but for the hallways of the entire school.

These gatherings brought us, boys and girls alike, into an informal, safe setting, focused on a common goal – decorating the school for Christmas. We were, of course, already excited about the season, and the work was fun as well. But soon these gatherings – by design, I think – evolved into small, informal social events. Somehow, a record player appeared, and we soon started to bring our favorite 45s, as Mr. Ireland's after school arts and crafts sessions gave way to miniature sock hops.

While not my original reason for attending – the artwork and the opportunity to hang out with a nice group of kids was enough – the best thing about all of this was April, with whom I always seemed to be partnered for the work, and soon enough, for the dancing as well.

The song to which we danced most often, because we requested it be played often enough to wear out the grooves on the record, was "Mr. Blue" by the Fleetwood's. So, as Gary crooned, and Gretchen and Barbara harmonized, April and I would hold each other – to an appropriate 13-year-old degree, of course – and glide away the afternoon. It was my first "our song," and as the saying goes, you never forget your first.

Senior High School 1960 – The Big Time

A Brand New Freshman

Early in September of 1960, along with 300 and some odd others, I took a giant step upward and became a freshman at Aurora East Senior High School, the last ninth grade class, in fact, to be at the high school level.

When I arrived at East High for the first day of classes, I was resplendent in black slacks and a bright red button-down twill shirt. The school colors, announcing to one and all that I knew where I was, and that I had school spirit, and that I most certainly was a brand new freshman. Actually, if I was noticed at all by anyone, it was with humor or derision. But I soldiered on through the day.

First to homeroom, where I met our homeroom teacher, Miss Schmidt, whose name changed the following year to Mrs. Hess, and the classmates with whom I would share the morning ritual for the next four years.

Homerooms at the senior high level were organized alphabetically and two of my grade school friends were there, Mark Siebers and Stanley Seton, as well as my former junior high dancing partner, April. Unbeknownst to me, my future best friend, Vern Schramer, just missed the cut. A girl on whom I would have a bit of a crush for the next school year did make the cut.

Soon after finding out where this girl lived – just far enough away to have gone to a different grade school – I rode my bike down her street a couple of times after school, in the early autumn evenings. I had terrible luck with that bicycle, for it seemed that each time I approached her house, I would suffer some sort of mechanical breakdown, causing me to stop and investigate the problem. As I was peering intently at the mechanism, she would emerge from her front door and come over to find out what was the matter.

At just about that point, the problem would magically correct itself, leaving us free to talk for the next 15 minutes or so, probably under the watchful eyes of what I would later come to realize were very strict parents.

Swimming in Gym Class

Aside from a new homeroom, meeting the girl of my adolescent dreams, and my eye-catching apparel, the only other thing I remember about my first day at East High was physical education, or "gym" class. Our gym teacher for that semester was the likable Joe Maze, one of the school's old-timers and assistant football coach, famous for his lisping encouragement to "Huthel boys, huthel."

As I stood among the rather odd collection of boys comprising Mr. Maze's first semester freshman gym class, not only was roll called, but the curious question, "Why are you here?" was asked. As we progressed, each boy cited some malady, from clubfoot, to poor eyesight, to obesity – a rarity in those days. When my name was called, I was embarrassed to confess that I did not know why I was there. Mr. Maze paused and wrote a note beside my name – which, of course, singled me out amongst this group of strangers – and then moved on.

A brief after class investigation revealed that I was in the class by mistake, but schedules being set, I might as well remain in "Special Class" until the end of the semester. There was an up-side to this confusion, however. Each gym class rotated every three weeks through various activities – basketball, gymnastics, archery, baseball (in season), and others, including swimming in the school's rather nice pool, adjacent to the gymnasium. Whether planned or the luck of the draw, I don't know, but Special Class was first in the pool. So, for my first three weeks at Aurora East High School, I went swimming every day.

Wrestling – Sort of

One of my first semester classes in freshman year at East High was mechanical drawing/drafting. Not really knowing any better, I focused on the word "drawing" and eagerly signed up. I was mistaken, however; the mechanical part and the /drafting part combined to make this, in reality, a class on the drawing of blueprints and such. This proved to be another example of the serendipity that seemed to often guide my life. Though not something in which I had an interest – or really even knew of – the ability to read, and to create detailed, accurate sketches, as well as part and concept drawings, albeit at an amateur level, served me very well as the years rolled forward.

The drafting teacher was Mr. Gavonni who, drafting aside, was passionate about two issues of which he made us well aware. One, it was absolutely forbidden for a shirttail not be tucked neatly into your slacks, and the other was wrestling. Mr. Gavonni was also the assistant wrestling coach, and as such, was quite enthusiastic about extolling the virtues of the wrestling team.

So, when October and the football season ended more or less

simultaneously, I signed up for the wrestling team. There, I struggled as a mediocre to average wrestler, and worked hard at staying below 180 pounds, the last weight before the unlimited heavyweight class. This was made considerably more difficult by my mother's cooking.

But I liked the team, the one-on-one "Mano-a-Mano" format, and – despite a lack of any real talent on my part – the sport itself. On the downside, my frequent practice partner that first year was a fellow named Washington, a senior tackle on the football team, already bound for the University of Illinois on a full football scholarship, and who seemed – to me anyway – to be twice my size. This usually reduced my participation in practice to that of a crash dummy as my "partner" tossed me about while honing his skills.

In the process, I did, however, manage to learn a few things, and as a freshman, I felt honored to be working on a daily basis with one of the school's athletic stars.

Meeting Vern

Halfway through my freshman year at East High, I met a curious fellow named Vern Schramer. I think I was seated next to him in one class or another and we got on well enough within that context, but no big deal. Then, one cold winter evening, a Tuesday I oddly enough seem to remember, I ran across him at the Buy-Rite market near my house. We decided, spur-of-the-moment, to go out and cause some trouble. That's not how it was framed, of course, but it was what seemed to happen when Vern and I got to gallivanting through the streets of Aurora. Not real trouble; just mischief (small "m"). The kind of thing that the person on the receiving end was often quite unhappy with, and everyone else would write off as "boys will be boys."

On this night, it turned out that Vern had some firecrackers and, wonder of wonders, a book of matches. It was quickly decided that it would be great fun to toss lit firecrackers onto front porches in the neighborhood. We accomplished the tossing part well enough, but since it was cold and damp, and a little snowy, none of the firecrackers actually went off. One did, however, bounce off the front picture window of a house. The owner immediately came out through the front door, saw it lying on his porch, and gave chase.

It turned out that Vern was much better at escaping than I was. Between the houses we ran, only to encounter a fence with a latched gate. In a flash, Vern was up and over the fence and gone into the night. As I was considering how to get over the fence, I was nabbed. I managed to convince the man that,

1) I was a pretty good guy. That *other* fellow, the one with the firecrackers and all the bad ideas, was some kid I had just met that night, and I didn't even know his name, "Honest Mister", and

2) I lived not too far away and my dad was an upstanding citizen, and

3) The guy was probably getting cold and realized he had no real complaint to lodge. So, he let me go with a stern warning.

Elmer's Dog House

Another special time in my early adolescence, for no discernible reason whatsoever, was the late winter and early spring of 1961. With a whole semester at East High behind me, I had new friends and knew my way around, but aside from that, it all just seemed special; and seeming so at the time, it remains so in my memory today.

And what I remember most is the music. Like all of my

friends, I listened to WLS radio where disc jockey Dick Biondi and others played what came to be some of my favorite songs, one after another. Hearing such songs as "Wonderland by Night" by Bert Kaempfert and His Orchestra, "Corrina, Corrina" by Ray Peterson, "Apache" by Jorgen Ingmann, and " Theme From Exodus" by the twin pianos of Ferrante and Teicher, and many others, will pull me powerfully back to that time.

I envision ice skating at Phillips Park, hanging out at the lunch counter at Kressge's, a downtown dime store which would slowly disappear, only to reemerge a decade later as Kmart. And oddly, a strong, clear memory of riding with my mother on Friday evenings to pick up the family's takeout fish dinners from "Elmer's Dog House" on Farnsworth Avenue, and of hearing – on the car's radio – songs which I will always remember, including "Blue Moon" by The Marcels, and *My Absolute, All Time, Number One Favorite Song*, "Will You Still Love Me Tomorrow" by the Shirelles.

Vern Again – and Always

But time is fleeting. Late winter becomes late spring, and the final bell rang out. Freshman year was over, and a wonderfully long, schedule-free summer lay before me.

One morning in June, I was looking for something to do so I decided to visit Bill K____, an acquaintance from the recent school year who I had bumped into somewhere the week before, and with whom I spent a fun afternoon.

A curious place where he lived with his mother, his home was a very large house on 4th Street, which you entered, climbed to the second floor, and walked the hallway to his door, which opened into a small suite of rooms. Each door in the corridor, I was told, led to a similar suite in which strangers lived. I had theretofore never seen or heard of such a thing. But I accepted it without comment, and now knowing how to get there, I mounted my bicycle and off I went. I never made it.

As I set off, riding my bike to Bill's, hoping he would be at home, I rounded the corner from Weston Avenue onto 4th Street. There, a guy on a bicycle, about my age, came out of a driveway between two houses, carefully balancing several yard tools – rake, shovel, etc. – on the handlebars. It was that fellow Vern, whom I had encountered on a cold Tuesday night last winter at the Buy-Rite, ironically, just a few doors from where we now were.

We stopped to talk, and I discovered that this was his aunt's house, and that he had been doing some yard work, and would I help him get his bulky tools back to his house, a couple of blocks away. My earlier mission was forgotten as I said "sure." And that's how it all began.

Vern and I quickly became best friends, a relationship which remained virtually unchanged until he passed away. The only difference – an evolution really – is that I count his family, wife, and grown children as close friends as well.

A few years after Vern and I met, Simon and Garfunkel would release the album, *Bookends*, and the song, "Old Friends," which tells of two friends sitting quietly on a park bench, remembering old times, and wondering how they somehow got to be 70 years old.

Although I never spoke of it, I recall projecting forward, in my mind's eye, and thinking that someday in the far, far distant future this would be Vern and me.

And now, although we will never have the chance to share that quiet time together, and 70 looms large on a not too distant horizon, I think of how we started, and of the song, and increasingly, of my old friend.

Ken Schramer's Younger Brother

My father worked as a first shift machinist at Thor Power Tool Company. When the second shift began at 3:30 pm, another machinist, often younger and less experienced, would take over and keep the machines running and producing until midnight.

In the spring of 1961, my father had commented more than once on his new "Night Man" named Ken. A nice young fellow, smart, hardworking, and with plenty of good old-fashioned common sense, my dad thought a lot of Ken Schramer. So, when I showed up at home one day with my new best friend, Vern – with the same last name – my dad's first, and surprising, question was, "You're not Ken's brother, are you?" Indeed he was, and from that moment on, in my father's eyes, Vern could do no wrong, an attitude which benefited me greatly as the years passed, and "wrong" we would occasionally do.

Vern Schramer's Older Brother

Vern worshiped his older brother, Ken. Five years older than we were, I remember Ken as the ideal teenager of his time. Not the crew-cut all-American quarterback type, but rather a milder version of "Fonzie." Good-looking, friendly, with a very fast, very cool car – a souped-up '58 Plymouth Fury – and a streak of mischief which seems to run in the family, Ken was worthy of imitation, and imitate him we did.

We affected his mannerisms and style. At the time Vern and I met, Ken jauntily wore a "Castro-style" fatigue cap. A quick trip to the Army-Navy surplus store and Vern and I had such hats for ourselves, which we wore all that summer. As we each became part of the other's family, I soon looked up to Ken as a sort of ersatz big brother.

Ken had a circle of friends who covered a large portion of the very far western suburbs – there was a lot of corn between Aurora and the actual western suburbs in 1961. A focal point of Ken's social circle was Chobar's Restaurant, a country diner in the middle of nowhere, but central geographically to the group.

Chobar's Restaurant was notched into a cornfield on the southwest corner of the crossing of Illinois Routes 59 and 65, which today is one of the busiest intersections in the state, surrounded by malls, condos, car dealers, and a very large medical center.

When I'm in the area, I'm sometimes reminded of those infrequent occasions when Ken let us "ride along" and we could hang out with the older kids. And when we did so, Vern and I would be delighted at how cool we were.

My one regret, as winter drew near, was that my new best friend didn't ice skate.

Ice Skating – Part 3 – Gang Tag and Girls

As I previously mentioned, my favorite winter activity throughout junior high, senior high, and that last winter before I left for the Navy, was ice skating. And it was also on the Phillips Park lagoon that my social circle widened considerably.

Although Phillips Park lay on the far eastern edge of town, the lagoon was, sort of automatically, neutral territory in the intra-city rivalry which I believe still exists between those on the east and west sides of the Fox River.

Author's Note: The annual football game between the East and West High Schools, the capstone of every season, is the oldest high school football rivalry in the country, and until sometime after World War II was played on Hurd's Island, a "no man's land" in the middle of the

river. Even now, meeting someone who turns out to be
from Aurora always sparks the inevitable question,
"Which Side?"

But on the lagoon, it didn't seem to matter. Girls, from any-where, were accepted automatically, and boys were judged, at least initially, on their ability to skate, and if they played "Gang Tag."

This was important, for besides paying attention to and attracting the attention of the girls, our principal on-ice activity was a game called Gang Tag. Flirting with the girls was general-ly better done in the comfort of the hothouse, and skating serenely across the ice with them didn't generate enough activity to ward off the cold – unless there weren't enough guys to start a game. Then, of course, we would skate with the girls – and always manage somehow to stay warm enough.

Ice Skating – Part 4 – Playing Gang Tag

The game of Gang Tag, which we played almost obsessively on the ice of the Phillip's Park lagoon, was actually quite simple. One person would be IT*, the first "Chaser," and would begin the game by skating to the far end of the oval and returning, while everyone else just sort of drifted to the center. As IT turned back toward the center and started to give chase, the game was on. The goal was to tag another player, a "Runner," who upon being tagged, also became a Chaser and the two of them set out to tag others, and so on. The game ended when the last runner – pursued with vigor by *everyone* else – was tagged.

---

* *"Chaser" and "Runner" are terms I've created to describe player designa-tions and roles. These terms were never used in a game – we just knew. The designation "IT" is universal.*

This was great fun for all; both Chasers *and* Runners, and so every game presented me with a decision. To be tagged first meant you were "IT" for the next game, and sometimes I would offer myself up to be tagged first, and would thus be a Chaser for two full games. Usually though, I would try desperately, and quite often successfully, to be among the last to be tagged. It required skill, speed, and no small amount of recklessness, to evade 15 or 20 guys who, at that moment, cared for nothing more than to place a not too gentle hand upon you, and yell "Tag!"

Of course, the evasion was just as single-minded. We mostly all had racing skates and the speeds we achieved were really quite remarkable, as was the maneuverability; we had blades which were not designed for the quick stops, turns, and cut-backs often required to pursue or to get away. The girls were not part of the game, and were, of course, completely immune from the rough play. But that didn't stop us from using them to involuntarily set a pick, knowing that a pursuer would have to maneuver carefully around them as the runner escaped in the other direction.

These mass, "gang" taggings often led to pileups in the closing moments of a game, with legs and bladed feet flying about, and with the ever present possibility of an inadvertent puncture wound. But this only happened once, as I recall, in all the games in which I played. Fortunately, a quick trip to the emergency room by the puncturee resulted in little more damage than not being able to skate for a couple of weeks.

Not an Athlete

I was grateful for my prowess on ice skates for reasons other than being a "star" Gang Tag player, and hopefully impressing the West High girls. With the exception of ice skating, I was really, although athletic, not a very successful athlete in my younger days – which, in the high school environment in which I existed, nicely complemented my lack of scholarship.

First of all, I could not run fast. For some reason, I just wasn't as fast as most of the other guys. A hip replacement some 30 years later, and the (very) slight misalignment problem which was determined to be the cause, eventually provided the answer as to why, when running wind sprints at football practice, and the last three guys always had to run an extra sprint, I was always one of them. The fact that I was miles ahead of the other two sprinters counted for nothing. All that mattered was that I was one of the "slow guys."

I might've been pretty good at football – my brother certainly was – except for my lack of speed, and the fact that my class ('64) at East High produced, truly, one of the greatest teams in the school's history. This provided many thrilling victories, all of which I got to watch.*

I had *no* basketball skills whatsoever and, at that time consequently was not much of a fan of the game. And in track, I could run very well, just not very fast. The strength events, shot put, discus, and so on, were dominated by the same fellows who were the All-State lineman on the football team. That left baseball; still America's pastime in those days, in which every boy dreamed of being a star and of hitting a Series winning home run to beat the Yankees.

And I could hit!! From Little League age onward, I could be reliably counted upon to put the bat on the ball. But alas, as a fielder, I sucked. The outfield, again due to lack of speed, was out of the question, and catching didn't look to be *any* fun at all. But I did have the quickness and reflexes for the infield, except for one fatal flaw – I was afraid of the ball.

---

* *I would make up for this to some degree a decade later by being, I think, a very good football referee.*

Every infielder knows of the "bad hop" which could put the sharply hit baseball squarely on your nose, and lurks, potentially, just one play in the future; and if you can't put that out of your mind and just play, you can't play very well. Plus, in all honesty, I didn't have a strong enough arm to effectively play any further around the horn than second base.

But I *could* hit! And I maintain that had there been the "designated hitter" in Little League in 1955, I would be in the Hall of Fame today. Oh well, I could skate pretty good. This led me eventually to another of life's truths – be really good at *something* and don't fret too much over the rest.

"Spinout at Sebring"

I have previously mentioned how enthralled we were with TV, and that I was influenced by a single episode of a popular show.

In the late 1950s, *77 Sunset Strip* was a very popular TV program, and set the standard for a number of future such shows. The format was simple; a small group of private eyes had an office in a glamorous location, which was often the title of the program. The cast would include a secretary, either glamorous or cute depending on the program, and an offbeat P. I. wannabe who would invariably be involved, somehow, in the weekly adventures. Opening shots of the glamorous locale and a catchy theme song rounded out the package.

A couple of years later, one such show, this one located in Miami Beach, was *Surfside 6*. In strict adherence to the format, the PIs had an office aboard a large houseboat moored at, you guessed it, Surfside No. 6. Actually the houseboat's true location was a canal beside Collins Avenue, across from the Fontainebleau Hotel, but you can't make a title or a good theme song, out of that.

The offbeat character in this drama was the handsome, dashing, and wealthy young Sandy Winfield II, played by current heartthrob, Troy Donahue. Sandy was a dilettante, with enough money to indulge himself in any activity he chose. But he was a likable sort, and in fact, the star of the show.

In the May 8, 1961 episode, "Spinout at Sebring," Sandy, also an amateur sports car racer, was offered the opportunity to co-drive a Ferrari Testa Rossa in the annual 12-hour endurance race for sports cars at Sebring, Florida. The episode, culminating of course in the race itself, included many clips taken from the actual race of beautiful and exotic cars sliding around tight turns, and blasting down the straights. And watching this episode unfold, I was hooked. The scenes of the race, as well as those in the garage, with mechanics tuning the highly sophisticated and powerful Ferrari, were, in all probability, the proximate cause of my abandoning electronics for engine mechanics a year or so later.

A Ferrari Fan Forever

I would soon learn that the *"12 hours of Sebring"* was the first event of an annual series of international races, mostly in Europe, which determined the world championship for sports/racing cars. Dominated by the works teams of Ferrari, Maserati, Jaguar, and Porsche, among others, this was the big time. The notion that a private entry, driven by an amateur, could win the race was beyond plausibility. But it *was* exciting and compelling to someone not knowledgeable in the sport, and at the time, I certainly was not.

But not for long. The next time I found myself in Shindle's Pharmacy, I bypassed the comic book rack in favor of the magazines. There I discovered *Road & Track, Car and Driver,* and *Sports Car Graphic,* which between them covered all of the major racing events in Europe and North America. It was here that I discovered, and developed, a lifelong passion for small, fast cars, for sports car racing, and for the ultimate of motor-sports, Formula One.

It happened that Ferrari dominated the racing world in 1961, and because of Sandy's fanciful drive in the Testa Rossa, I was already predisposed to favor the bright red cars from Maranello. And so I became, and still am, a solid Ferrari fan – a "Tifosi", as us fanatical Ferrari fans are known worldwide. That year the "big" Testa Rossas, Ferrari's last front engine racecars, were nearly unbeatable, as were that year's Formula One cars; the now famous F-156 Sharknose, which remains my all-time favorite automobile, along with its sports/racing counterpart, the new rear-engine 246 SP – really just an F1 car with two seats, fenders, and larger engine.

The Death of a Hero

As the 1961 European auto racing season progressed, I followed along in the only way available – through the maga-zines, with race reporting trailing the actual events by as much as a month. With a couple of notable exceptions, Ferrari dom-inated both sports car and Formula One racing. And although the Ferrari team included Phil Hill, a Californian who was to become the first American world champion, I became a fan of his teammate and F1 rival, Count Wolfgang Graf Berghe "Taffy" von Trips, a German aristocrat who was also a world-class racing driver.

In September, toward the end of the season, and before the next month's magazine issues were out, a tiny *Beacon News* arti-cle in the back of the sports pages reported in matter-of-fact fashion that, in the penultimate race of the season, the Italian Grand Prix at Monza, Italy, Ferrari driver, Wolfgang von Trips fatally crashed, thus propelling race winner, Phil Hill, to the

1961 World Drivers Championship.

And I was devastated. Reading those two small paragraphs reminded me sharply of reading the similarly understated article telling of the death of Buddy Holly and the others on the day the music died, and I felt a similar sense of sorrow, loss, and rage. A number of years later, I visited the racetrack at Monza and stood at the spot where Taffy's car struck the embankment and tragically tumbled into the crowd, and relived the emotions of a boy who had lost a hero.

But the music didn't die, it just paused a moment, and moved on. And Ferrari – although having already won the championship and choosing not to participate in the last race of the season – would go on to win many more races, win more championships, and yes, lose more drivers. There's another of life's lessons in there somewhere, but I just can't put it into words.

My First Job

I got my first job in the summer of 1961 at Aurora Cleaners and Furriers where my mother, my father, and both of my aunts had worked at one time or another. In fact, my Aunt Mary continued to work there, and would do so until she passed away some 25 years later. So it was sort of a family tradition.

The job responsibilities were diverse, but simple. The principal task during the workday was to "make up hangers." This meant placing a foam rubber strip onto a metal clothes hanger and putting it onto a stack, and to then deliver these stacks to the garment pressers who, in turn, used them up at an impressive rate. This, as well as running miscellaneous errands and doing chores, kept me quite busy during the day.

At the end of the day, when the pressers and others went home, I stayed. I emptied all of the trash containers, and thoroughly swept the entire floor. As I said, simple. I also occasionally assisted – to the level of my ability – with maintenance tasks performed by a fellow named Jim, who was the one-man maintenance crew, and general all-around handyman. He was originally from somewhere in the South and had an odd accent. But he was friendly, good at his job, and I found him to be interesting, entertaining, and quite willing to teach me things about the mechanics of his job and, a year later, on the rebuilding of an old six-cylinder automobile engine.

The "finishing" area where I spent most of my time was on the second floor of the old building. It was here that cleaned or laundered garments were steam-pressed, hung, and bagged. They were then conveyed to the first-floor holding area, and from there returned to the customers, either by delivery or via the front counter. And the circle was complete.

The hanger station – actually just a table with stacks of hangers and foam strips – was in the center of the finishing area, surrounded by presses and other machinery, which were constantly belching steam into the atmosphere. On a typical summer day, the term "hot and humid" didn't begin to describe the working atmosphere in which these people – and I – worked. But it was a good job which paid real money, and one which I would not have, had it not been for my family connection. I could, and did, live with the heat.

Plus, at the hanger table, I could listen to the radio while I worked, and as I did so, the musical magic of 1961 continued on into the summer. In those days, the only radio station to listen to was WLS; Clark Weber in the morning, Art Roberts in the afternoon, and in the evenings Dick Biondi, Chicago's star DJ at the time. And it was at "my" hanger table that I kept my stack of WLS Silver Dollar Surveys. These sheets, perhaps 4" x 10", contained the top 40 songs of the week, the top album, and of course a bit of advertising, promoting one DJ or another. They were available in any quantity you wanted, for free at any record store in town. But keeping track of the music was important; and, besides, it was cool to have a complete set.

Coke Bottles

In my job at Aurora Cleaners, while I worked at my hanger table, I could slowly consume a small bottle of "ice cold" Coke, obtained for five cents from the vending machine near the stairs. An annoying aspect of this, however, was that the owner's son, who was the principal delivery driver, about my mother's age, and who knew my mother and my aunts quite well, complained that I always had a bottle of Coke at my table, and was, therefore, consuming mass quantities of the stuff. This did not please my mother, and as with other things, displeasure rolls downhill. When confronted, I tried to explain that I was sipping the stuff, and could make a bottle of Coke last a long time. But no one seemed to believe me. Very frustrating.

Besides, with what I was being paid, where in the world did they think I would be getting all those nickels?

The Freshman Clique

Aside from a very good football team, my class produced the biggest collection of elitists and snobs the school has perhaps ever seen. In 1961, the so-called "Freshman Clique" was so socially powerful at the school that even the seniors complained. They managed to take the notion of the popular, or cool, kids to another level, and it was a group in which I had no part.

I, instead, fell into the social limbo which lies somewhere between the student elite and the school's "bad element," but was more likely to associate with the latter. The Clique, including some former friends, was not very inclusive of those who fell short somehow.

A few years later, I would be a member of just such a group, on a much smaller scale. That I would cherish my status within that future group to the extent that I did was, I'm sure, influenced by this earlier rejection.

Friday Night Dances at the "Y"

Beginning (for me anyway) in the spring of 1961 and on until I left for the Navy, virtually every Friday night was spent, for at least part of the evening, at a dance somewhere.

At first, the venue for these events was always the "new" YMCA on the west side of town. The old "Y" on the corner of Fox (now East Downer) and LaSalle Streets, where I learned to swim (naked), and to socialize with boys from all over town, was closed in favor of the new facility. The new Y, in which I never swum a lap, had not only a nice pool but a large gymnasium where there was plenty of room on Friday evenings for girls to dance, and for most of the boys to lean against the walls. Sometimes the boys would stroll around the perimeter of the dance area, gazing inward, Wishin' and Hopin', and sometimes, might even take the plunge, but . . .

The music was heard from the gym's PA system and was supplied by a guy with a stack of 45s and a phonograph set up on a small table just inside the entrance. It was, of course, contemporary; Del Shannon, Dion, The Lettermen, the Bobbies, Rydell and Vee, and so forth. By 1963, it was largely British music with the Beatles and the Stones prominent, but with the likes of Herman's Hermits, Peter and Gordon, and even Freddy & the Dreamers in the rotation. But no matter the year, the last song of the night was always the beautiful (slow dance) instrumental, "Theme from a Summer Place" by Percy Faith and His Orchestra.

Hearing this song signaled, in the earlier years, an impending long walk home or, as the years passed, a trip to Prince Castle, Burger Chef, or Tops Drive-In in someone's car. I didn't dance to this song anywhere near as often as I would've liked. The girls, it seemed, followed the advice of the Drifters and Saved the Last Dance for . . . whomever they were going, or wanted to be going, with. And if you were there with the guys, it was sometimes tough to end the evening on a high note.

Record Hop – On Stage with the "Wild I-tralian"

Beside the weekly Friday night events at the Y and the CYA, I went to several sock hops or dances which featured well-known bands, or were hosted by a popular DJ, or sometimes both. One such event was held in a Catholic school gym somewhere – my aging memory suggests that it was in Aurora's "Pidgeon Hill" neighborhood, but I may be wrong. But in any event, it was well outside my normal sphere of travel at the time.

On this autumn evening in my high school years, I went alone for some reason to such a dance. The highlight of the night was the MC of the event, Dick Biondi, none other than the star DJ of the best radio station in the world, WLS in Chicago. This last is just my opinion, but not by any means a singular view.

I had a nice time that night; I saw a few friends and met a few new people. Aside from the music, the dancing, and the clever patter of the MC, there were "Special Guests" and other entertainment planned for the teenage crowd. One of these required a boy and girl to come up on stage to compete in some pop music related contest. This got everyone's attention. Not the prize so much as the possibility of actually standing on the stage with Dick Biondi himself.

As Dick kept up the chatter, one of his minions scanned the audience for the contestants. After a moment or two, he stopped scanning and pointed straight at ME, gesturing and saying "come on up." I was so shocked at being selected, as well as the thought of actually standing on stage with the guy that I had largely come here just to see, that I hesitated. Perhaps I hesitated a moment too long, for as I was getting myself moving through the throng and to the steps at the side of the stage, he selected another boy, and then a girl. So, in due course, all three of us arrived on stage. This result, I'm sure, disrupted, to some degree, an otherwise carefully laid plan. For my part, I immediately took the decision that if there were one too many kids on stage, that *I* had been chosen, and chosen FIRST. And so I was staying right where I was – standing on stage next to Dick Biondi for all to see.

I'm sure the careful plan included contingencies for all manner of unexpected happenstance. The contest went off without a hitch, and we were soon back on the floor among the others. The evening moved on and eventually ended. Well, almost. It was announced that Dick Biondi would be in the cloakroom signing autographs for a short period of time.

So I joined the crowd until I finally reached the counter of the split cloakroom door and there he was. When it was my turn, I handed over a piece of paper for Dick to sign, hoping he would remember speaking to me during our brief onstage encounter. He did not. But that was okay. I left and went home feeling that, all in all, I had had a pretty good night.

Geometry Class – Fini Mathematics

I've spoken of my habit of doodling sometimes as a method of "staying in the room," be it a classroom or a business meeting. A somewhat different, but relevant example of this occurred during my sophomore year at East High.

I'm the first to admit that I have limited "mathematical aptitude." In spite of this, I fared well enough in algebra class as a freshman. One year of basic algebra was the extent of the mathematics requirement at my high school, but having passed easily enough, I signed up for sophomore geometry.

Geometry turned out to be somewhat simple, but for me not at all engaging. I nonetheless passed the first semester without significant effort. I credit this to the fact that I had friends in class, with whom I occasionally joked and mildly misbehaved. This, I'm convinced, is what kept me in the classroom; joking around notwithstanding, I paid enough attention to pass with a grade of "C."

With the change of semester, the classroom roster changed and I found myself without friends in geometry class. My mind now free to wander, I missed most of what was said to me in class and I, therefore, failed. And subject to the rule of the time, failing the second semester caused me to fail the entire year. I readily admit that the fault lay with me, and the net result was, while the first semester marked the high point, the second semester of sophomore geometry marked the *end* of my mathematics training.

Second Plymouth - First Drive

In the summer of 1962, between my sophomore and junior years at East High, my parents briefly owned three cars. The venerable '50 Plymouth was relegated to "Dad's car" in favor of a sleek, and much more modern, '58 Chevy, now the official family car which my mother also used for everyday travel. Somehow, a third car appeared, a second Plymouth sedan – a '51 I think, and blue – but otherwise virtually identical to the '50 with which I was now quite familiar. Not privy to, nor really caring about, the details of the acquisition or the disposition of this car, I don't know how all of this happened, but soon after it was acquired, it was sold to Jim, the maintenance man at Aurora Cleaners.

Jim planned to drive the car, but decided first to rebuild the engine. So one weekday afternoon, Jim and I took our leave from the cleaners to move the car to his house. I didn't know the plan, but was happy to be away from the hanger table for a couple of hours, so off we went. When we got to my house, Jim handed me the keys to his "new" car and instructed me to follow him home. Immediately, conflicting emotions were at war inside my head.

I did know how to drive. I had briefly taken the wheel under my father's watchful eye, on more than a few country roads on our family after-dinner rides, but I was still 15 years old and did not have a permit, let alone a driver's license. I looked at him as if he were crazy, but inside, the excitement was building. I was actually going to drive a car, alone, through the streets of Aurora.

It was a distance of about two miles, and the trip went quickly and without incident. I know my parents would've been furious had they found out, but I will always cherish the experience of my first "solo" drive.

For the balance of that summer, I spent a fair amount of my free time helping Jim rebuild that engine. This was performed mostly in Jim's garage, and on tables set up in his driveway. It was crude, but engines were simpler in those days and Jim knew what he was doing. I not only enjoyed the work, but learned a lot. The experience furthered my already keen interest in engines, and cars in general, and helped lead me to Engineman School when I joined the Navy.

The Five Esses

Aside from an occasional disagreement, during which we wouldn't speak for a couple of days, Vern was far and away my closest friend. From the day we met, this was, and remained, a lifelong constant. But for a short while, in our middle high school years, it was not just Vern and me, but a slightly larger group.

Vern had met, and befriended, a fellow named Dennis S. who was a year older and had both a driver's license and an actual car – a '51 Plymouth. And then we were three; and a now mobile three, at that. At about that same time, I introduced Vern to my old grade school, and current homeroom friend, Mark S. And three became four. Occasionally joined by Dennis' friend, Jerry S., we were now a group (or perhaps a gang, though more in the old-time sense of *Our Gang* than what the term implies today). We even had a cool, if somewhat obvious, name for ourselves; "The Five Esses," and with matching jackets we were, or so we imagined, just too cool for words.

My memory suggests that we, as a group, spent more of our Friday nights at the CYA dances than at the "Y." These events were held in the gym/theater on the second floor of the Knights of Columbus building at Lincoln Avenue and Galena – conveniently right across the street from Prince Castle (good burgers and great ice cream), and just down the block from the original "hole in the wall" Don Walker's Sandwich Center (absolutely the best Italian beef sandwiches on the planet, then or now).

But the main attractions of the CYA functions were that the place was small, compared to the "Y," and more importantly, that it was popular with a lot of girls. We would cruise in, sporting our fancy jackets, hair neatly combed, breath newly freshened by Binaca, hoping to make an impression. This we usually did, and occasionally, a favorable one.

We would circle the perimeter, just as at the "Y" – although a complete lap took a lot less time – and even danced now and then to songs like *The Way You Look Tonight* by The Lettermen, *Close To Cathy* by Mike Clifford, or *What Would My Mary Say?* by Johnny Mathis.

I know they played a fair number of up-tempo rock 'n roll songs as well, but for some reason, I mostly remember the gooey stuff. Maybe it was the dancing part.

The Music of My Time – Random Thoughts

My transition to junior high school in 1958 was also about the same time that I was becoming aware of, and increasingly interested in, the popular music of the day, and the dominant music of the demographic into which I was now entering was, of course, rock 'n roll.

For the most part, early rock 'n roll was an uncomplicated music, at least from the listener's perspective. Sure there were back-up singers, and a lot of orchestration in some of the hit songs – mostly violins it seemed – but to start a band, all that was really required was the tried and true four-person formula; lead and rhythm guitars, bass, and drums. Or simpler yet, a few guys and an acoustic guitar, or maybe just some guys standing on a south Philly street corner singing a cappella.

As to the singers, there was Elvis of course, Bill Haley and his Comets. Buddy Holly, Freddy "Boom Boom" Cannon, Bobby Rydell, and the like. There were the ballads of Connie Francis, The Lettermen, and Brenda Lee, and the upbeat songs of Dodie Stevens, Paul Evans, and The Playmates (*Beep, Beep*); and the teen idols, such as Frankie Avalon, Dion DiMucci, and of course, Ricky Nelson.

Rock 'n roll instrumentals included the guitars of Duane Eddy, Santo & Johnny, The Virtues, and the Ventures. And, lest we forget, there were a few orchestral holdovers from prior times; Percy Faith, Perez Prado, Al Caiola, the beautiful, but lesser-known, *Our Winter Love* by Bill Pursell and His Orchestra, and always Henry Mancini's *Moon River*.

As time moved along, as it always does, the music was changing, as it also always does; but it was a slow evolution and hardly noticed. And then something happened. On a Friday evening in September 1963, I was allowed to use the family car – the '58 Chevy – to go to the Y, or the CYA dance, or wherever Vern and I would decide to go. While driving to pick up my friend, I was of course listening to WLS on the car's radio. During a break from the music, and the occasionally frantic patter of the DJ, I heard a very cryptic ad stating simply, "The Beatles are coming." I didn't know what that meant, so the phrase passed quickly through the conscious part of my brain. But it stuck somewhere because I do, in fact, remember quite clearly the time and place where I first heard mention of The Beatles.

From such innocuous and insignificant moments sometimes spring life-changing events, for soon the Beatles did come, bringing with them the rest of the British Invasion, and rock 'n roll – as we knew it – was dead. Actually, even before the Beatles, popular music (that is to say, the music of the young) was starting to splinter into many genres. In addition to the introduction of the Brits, which brought us everything from The Beatles and The Rolling Stones, to Petula Clark, Herman's Hermits, and Mary Hopkin, the homegrown stuff now suddenly seemed different as well.

It wasn't just rock 'n roll anymore. Hits like The Rooftop Singers' *Walk Right In* and *Washington Square* by The Village Stompers, and groups like the Kingston Trio gave a hint that folk music could join the mainstream. And so it was that traditional folk music, transitioned by the likes of Bob Dylan, and Phil Oches, Peter, Paul and Mary, and Simon and Garfunkel, became "folk rock" and was now a large part of the popular music scene.

Phil Spector changed American pop music forever with his "Wall of Sound," and with the girl groups of the 1960s; the Crystals, the Chiffons, the Shirelles, the Ronettes, and so on.

That old time rock 'n roll now had a theme; the music of the "Big Surf" and "Fast Cars" was rolling, or catching a wave. Spearheaded by the Beach Boys, the genre included Ronny and the Daytonas, The Rip Chords, and a lot of good stuff by Jan & Dean.

Doo-wop was gone, but Motown added a rich diversity, bringing R & B to everyone's transistor radio and phonograph, and introducing us to superstars, such as Smokey Robinson and the Miracles, the Temptations, the Supremes, and, oh, so much more.

And thank God for all of it. I've stated elsewhere in this narrative that I believe we are all defined, to a large degree, by the music we experience in a narrow band of years. For me, that time was the first half of the 1960s. What a grand musical era in which to come of age.

Final Years at East High 1963 – The Awakening

The Black Rose

In my junior year at East High, an event happened which marks the true beginning of my education, and as such, remains as perhaps the most significant turning point of my life. I learned to Read.

Not in the general sense; I could read to some degree, I'm told, since I was about five years old. But on this winter Sunday night in early 1963, I discovered the notion of reading for the pure pleasure of doing so. The trigger for this event was a movie I had just watched on TV; a swashbuckling tale of two twelfth-century Englishmen, who journeyed, via the Middle East and the Silk Road, to Cathay (China) and back again, experiencing many thrilling and romantic adventures along the way.

The Black Rose was the film adaptation of Thomas B. Costain's superb historical novel of the same name. Starring Tyrone Power as the young hero, and Orson Welles as the commanding general of Genghis Khan's army, even the movie version was breathtaking.

Built into the wall of our living room, near the stairs and

within sight of the room's most important feature – the TV, of course – was my mother's bookshelf. I had once or twice, on a boring afternoon, looked over the books therein, reading the curious titles of those thick, seemingly incomprehensible tomes. A tug at my memory caused me to check the bookshelf again and, sure enough, among my mother's novels was *The Black Rose*.

Before going to bed that night, I started to read the book, and was enthralled. The old cliché became literally (pardon the pun) true; I almost couldn't put it down, and it was this experience which led to my epiphany.

Good Books . . .

Prior to reading *The Black Rose*, I could read well enough, but other than comic books and auto racing magazines, I just didn't care; and to read a whole book seemed a chore and a bother.

Strangely enough though, I remembered that there *were* a couple of books which I had enjoyed in early grade school. The first, *Along the River Road* was a sort of Dick and Jane primer, supposedly written about nineteenth-century Aurora, though in the book they called it Hasting's Mill. A couple of years later, *If I Were Going* was a sort of combined literature *and* geography text, whose lessons were cleverly disguised as something in which I was actually interested.

The main characters, kids of course, and their teacher somehow traveled the world, visiting interesting places, and meeting peoples of many cultures. This book, it seems, has had a lasting influence. I have always wanted to visit the fjords of Norway because of that book. In another chapter, they all boarded a bus in England for a mystery tour. The teacher smiled, the driver "whistled a tantalizing tune," and they were off to St. Ives in Cornwall, a place I visited for the first time largely because of that book, and which has become a favorite destination. On occasion, when I take *If I Were Going* down from the shelf, I always read about St. Ives.

Yes, I have a copy, and it is a cherished possession.

. . . And Not So Good Books

After reading *The Black Rose*, I discovered the world of books, and also recalled books I had actually enjoyed in the past. But, I also had a couple of bad experiences regarding books. Very near the end of my fourth grade school year at Bardwell, I had not turned in a required final book report. I not only had not turned in a report, I had not read a book. I *had*, of course, read and reported on several books during the school year, but spring was upon us and I guess I just couldn't be bothered with this last assignment.

I was told that the penalty for failing to turn in the report was to not pass fourth grade, and to be held back for an encore performance next year. To a nine-year-old this is about the worst imaginable happenstance. But time was running out, and to compound my problem, the school library was closed, and so I was in something of a panic.

But fate stepped in, smiled briefly upon me, and a one-day delay in the deadline allowed me to go to the library, find a book, speed read it – without benefit of training, I might add – and write the report. Not a good report, I must admit, but acceptable. They didn't really *want* to hold me back, and aside from the book report, truly had no other reason to do so. But you can rail against cruel fate all you want; when you are nine years old, rules are rules.

In a reprise of my fourth grade experience, as the spring semester of sophomore English was drawing down, a final assignment was to read, and to report on, yes, a book. This situation was hauntingly familiar, and in fact, I *did* try. But in this case, it wasn't just any book, it was *Silas Marner* by George Eliot. Yes, I say again, I tried. But I'm not sure if there is a more ponderous and incomprehensible novel in the entirety of English literature than *Silas Marner*. And frankly, Victorian feminist writers would never come to be among my favorites.

It quickly became clear that this was, for me at least, an impossible task. With just days left, my teacher, in an effort to help, offered an alternative. However, in the few days I had left, A Tale of Two Cities turned out to be just as daunting, and the inevitable result was that I failed sophomore English; and by the rules of the day, not just the semester, but the entire year. I was given the choice of re-taking the course in summer school, or repeating all of sophomore English in my junior year, thus postponing the burden of summer school for a whole year. I chose the latter, and this, as I would come to realize, was a mistake.

A few years later, I discovered, to my dismay, that there were such things as "Cliff's Notes," which were readily available and offered a complete synopsis of whatever impossible reading task you might be assigned; in other words, a book report. My first thought, as I tipped my head and cried out to the heavens was, "Why didn't *anyone* tell me!"

Summer School – Junior English

So owing to my failure to pass sophomore English, and my foolish decision to not immediately repeat the course in summer school, I was required to take junior English in the summer session between my junior and senior years at East High. What I hadn't anticipated when I made the choice was my discovery of reading for pleasure. As it turned out, junior English was devoted entirely to creative writing, and since my "awakening," I've always regretted not taking this course for an entire school year.

The primary instructor of junior English was my homeroom teacher, now Mrs. Hess, so I felt a bit of a rapport, having been in her homeroom for every school day for three years. It turned out that I enjoyed the class very much, and having Mrs. Hess as the teacher helped greatly to make that so.

Having finally gotten started, I was reading a number of authors in those days; some good, some, in retrospect, not so much. I attempted *War and Peace* and *Wuthering Heights*, but decided to put them aside for later. I read all of the *James Bond* novels by Ian Fleming, the violence-filled mysteries of Mickey Spillane, and a number of mysteries by another author named Carter Brown. These last were, I confess, initially chosen for the sexy cover pictures on the paperbacks, but surprisingly turned out to be quite appropriate for a 16-year-old; not in content, so much, but in reading level.

So I was somewhat familiar with the mystery novel, and when the assignment was given to "write a short story," this was the genre I selected. I don't recall the title, and I didn't keep a copy, but the story itself was an old saw – a murder in an English manor house (Cretin Manor), with a number of suspects.

What I do recall was that in all likelihood it was absolutely dreadful. I also recall the effort I put into it. Realizing that I was required to lead the reader to the solution, rather than just announcing it on the final page, I spent a great deal of time attempting to insert various clues into the narrative. The exercise certainly gave me an appreciation for the effort and skill required to do what I had failed to do, to produce a *good* story.

The Grand Canal (of Mars)

At some point in my abbreviated junior year English class (taken in summer school), we were required to bring in and share a poem which we particularly liked. I suspect that for many in the class, finding a poem which spoke of anything more than the twinkling of little stars, was something of a challenge. To be honest, this would've been true of me as well, had I not read *The Black Rose*.

I'm sure that had I submitted a more current favorite, such as *The Mending Wall*, or the final stanza of *Dover Beach*, my choice would've been better received, but I was, at the time, reading my way through the science fiction works of Robert A. Heinlein, and so I chose instead a lyric from the fictitious Rhysling, bar room singer and "Poet Laureate of the Spaceways," titled the "Grand Canal of Mars".

"As Time and Space come bending back to shape this starspecked scene,
The tranquil tears of tragic joy still spread their silver sheen;
Along the Grand Canal still soar the fragile Towers of Truth;
Their fairy grace defends this place of Beauty, calm and couth.
Bone-tired the race that raised the Towers, forgotten are their lores,
Long gone the gods who shed the tears that lap these crystal shores.
Slow beats the time-worn heart of Mars beneath this icy sky;
The thin air whispers voicelessly that all who live must die.
Yet still the lacy Spires of Truth sing Beauty's madrigal;
And she herself will ever dwell along the Grand Canal.

"Permission granted by the
Robert A. & Virginia Heinlein Prize Trust,
care of Spectrum Literary Agency"

While accepted as a completed assignment, my choice was considered a bit too far from the mainstream. But poetry was new to me then and, outré or not, I liked it!

Joining the Navy?

One Friday morning in October of my senior year, I walked into homeroom and sat down beside my friend, Stanley. His first words to me that day were, "I joined the Navy last night, and you're going to join, too." After a couple of moments of mirthful amazement, I listened skeptically to what he had to say.

Stanley had a good friend whose father was a chief petty officer – of some aviation rating – in the reserve unit at Glenview Naval Air Station. As the first step in his father's footsteps, this friend had joined the reserves at the Aurora Armory, taking Stanley along.

I had grown up proud of my father's service, commanding a Sherman tank in World War II, and I'd always known that I would follow his example and be a soldier (for as long as the obligation lasted, anyway). This was enhanced to a large degree by watching *Combat* on TV, various WWII movies, and of course, by reading the comic book tales of *Sgt. Rock of Easy Company.*

But I'd also been influenced by my uncle who had been a gun mount captain on an aircraft carrier in the Pacific. And many of those war movies with which I grew up informed me that I also liked naval ships.

So this immediately available opportunity presented me with a dilemma. I had spent a fair portion of my youth re-creating, in my mind's eye, the "adventures" I imagined my father and his peers had had winning the "Good War," and knowing that one day I would also be a G. I. *(everyone – myself included – based my academic prowess on what I had demonstrated to this point, so college wasn't an issue).* But now, an altogether different future was presenting itself, and I decided that I at least owed it a fair hearing.

Having just achieved the age of 17, I was a free agent in the matter, so on the following Thursday evening, I met Stanley and together we went to the weekly meeting at the Naval Armory in Phillips Park. Perhaps it was a tactic, but once I was introduced to the appropriate people, I was treated as if I had arrived with my mind already made up. It was explained to me what I would be doing WHEN (not IF) I signed up, and where I *would* go, and what I *would* learn, and so on.

I was given, that very evening, the aptitude test which was then used by the Navy to evaluate potential enrollees. When I finished, I was told the number score that I had achieved. Having nothing to compare it to, this meant little to me, but I was told that it was a high score, one which would pre-qualify me for almost any service school which I *would* choose. This pleased me, but strangely – given my academic history – didn't surprise me. I knew I was a terrible student, but deep inside, I nonetheless *felt* that I was smart.

The result of this full-court press was that before Stanley and I left that evening, I was a member of the United States Naval Reserve. Serendipity again! Was this an impetuous decision? Yes. Did this have the potential to be a foolish decision? Yes. Did this turn out to be the right decision? Yes!

East High – The Final Year: Athletics

My last year at East High featured a mixed bag of athletics. My classmates were now the seniors on the '63 Tomcat football team and – supplemented, to some degree, by some of the more talented juniors – were totally, and completely, unbeatable; winning the inaugural year championship of the new Upstate Eight Conference, as they had won the final crown of the old Big Eight Conference the year before.

Sad to say, but I had given up on football a year prior. Not through lack of desire, or of not wanting to be a part of the team. But the team was just so damn good. My decision to leave was based on the reality that in this group, the time, effort, and the grueling practice schedule *(especially the brutal two-a-day sessions in August)* led only to the frustration of sitting on the bench until the last minute or so of home games, and the humiliation of never ever wearing an "away" jersey.

Still, I attended the games, and rooted for my former team-mates, and took pride in "the school's" accomplishments. But, I reasoned, if I were going to just watch, the view was better from the bleachers, and there were girls there as well.

To round out the year athletically, the basketball team was the yang to the gridiron yin. Several members of the wrestling team went to the state tournament and did well, but they had been there before so that was no surprise. The track & field and baseball teams were average, but unremarkable.

For me, as I have previously mentioned, "athletics" meant ice skating, where gang tag was not an IHSA sanctioned sport, unfortunately, but where I – I don't mind saying – was a standout.

East High – The Final Year: Academics

As the final football season of my high school years came to a close, my interest in East High athletics waned. At least for a while – I would be back before the decade was over, an East High alum and a rabid fan of both the football and basketball teams. But for now, my attention shifted to getting through the school year, and to the Navy, which lay just beyond. As I settled into my last year at East, it was evident, as it had been so all along, that while I got by, I would not excel in the high school environment. Not athletically, not scholastically, and not socially.

The Freshman Clique were now, of course, all seniors, and had complete control of the East High student society – their portion of it anyway. The rest of us just sort of did our own thing, and rode the continuum, waiting – for my part at least – for it finally to be over, and for life's next phase to begin.

The school year progressed as expected. The academic portion was, for me, actually no struggle at all; I just didn't work very hard at anything. Consequently, I concluded with a solid, well-deserved low C average. I was a bit wiser now, however. I knew what to do to not fail, and that was good enough. And in art class, the one thing I would normally look forward to, I was saddled with a teacher with whom I had no rapport, and for whom I had no respect.

There were exceptions, however, such as American history, in which I got an easy B. As usual, I expended no real effort, but the march of time, as presented by Mr. Davis, was both interesting and compelling – kind of like an adventure/drama story, but one whose conclusion remains, tantalizingly, just beyond the last page. In later years, I would wistfully regret, more than a few times, not pursuing a degree in, and a career teaching – and perhaps even writing – history. But at the time, such a notion would've seemed laughably far-fetched.

Given my previous experiences, both bad and good, with books, it was with extreme irony that I got through senior English to a large degree, it seemed, by reading novels. As I have previously noted, I had just recently discovered the pleasures of reading. My teacher was English Department Head Mr. Blackwell, whom I recall as being an okay guy – despite being old. But I didn't really get to know him very well for he had, that year, a student teacher who "assisted" in class. Actually, from my perspective, theirs was more like the relationship between a Professor and a T. A. In this case, the teacher hovered and observed, and I'm sure advised, but Professor-like, left most of the actual student contact to his protégé.

This earnest young fellow noted my interest in reading and encouraged me, recommending, and later discussing books which were, I now think, just a bit above my level, causing me to stretch a little without even knowing it. Thus, I slid through senior English doing mostly what I enjoyed, and only occasionally having to burden myself with such tedium as conjugating a verb, or diagramming a sentence.

I don't recall this young student teacher's name, but I'm quite sure that, if he didn't burn out somewhere along the line, he went on to a career as a great teacher. At least I hope so, for in a small, but significant way, he helped me as much as anyone to advance along the academic pathway.

But the real bright spot of each school day was Mr. Amyx's auto mechanics/metal workshop class, in a far corner of the lower floor, between the machinist's "classroom" and the print shop. It was to there that I migrated after my sudden and complete loss of interest in electronics – for I had heard the siren song of the internal combustion engine, and it was this classroom in which its secrets could be discovered.

It was there that I became part of a small group of "teacher's pets" who formed the team that participated in the annual Chrysler Corporation sponsored, interschool competition in automotive troubleshooting. We didn't win, but no matter, it was great fun and a very intense learning experience.

Those who continue to read this narrative will learn that, to no one's surprise, the school year ended *(not without some drama)* and I graduated, depositing me in an eventful, if somewhat surreal, period of my life, as everything in the following months was influenced to some degree by my impending departure for the US Navy.

East High – The Final Year: The Girl in the Office

As for teenage romance in my senior year at East High, the best opportunity for something special presented itself in September of 1963, an opportunity which I – being at the time a complete idiot and fool – totally wasted.

In the autumn of that year, there was a girl who started working in the office *(that is to say, the front end or customer service part)* of Aurora Cleaners where I still toiled, part-time, sorting and making up hangers, cleaning up after hours, and performing other such chores.

This new employee was my age, a senior at West High, and pretty, intelligent, sweet, and generally, as I saw her, a dream come true. After a short period of time, in which I took advantage of every excuse, real or imagined, to "go up front" and possibly talk with this girl, I mustered my courage and asked her out for a date – and she accepted.

We went to the Sandwich Fair, which I have always liked for its autumnal theme. We strolled about doing Sandwich Fair things. We looked at animals, both familiar and strange. I tried to win a bear *(I did not)*. We drank hot spiced cider, and rode the Tilt-O-Whirl, and all in all, had a rather nice time. Because the air was a bit nippy, we wore light jackets, and she wore a scarf, which she absentmindedly left in my car at the end of the evening.

Soon after, on a day when my recent date was not working, the ladies of the front office – all friends of my mother and my aunts – surrounded me and were questioning me closely about my date. When I mentioned the scarf, a wave of satisfaction rippled through the group. They began to chatter excitedly, saying that this was a tactic. That she wanted to see me again, and this was her way to ensure that I would call. The ladies were pleased. It was at just this point, however, when my being an idiot assumed control.

Rather than taking advantage of these invaluable allies, I instead somehow resented their involvement and vowed to myself that they weren't going to orchestrate me into some workplace romance, just for their own entertainment. The next day, I brought the scarf in and gave it to one of the ladies, asking her to please return it for me. And that was that!

I say again, for it certainly bears repeating, I was sometimes, and hope I am not too often, a complete fool.

The "Sixties" Begin

When I set forth for school that third Friday in November of my senior year at East High, I didn't know, along with everyone else, that the world was about to change. So much has been said about the death of John F. Kennedy that I certainly have little to add; other than to say, yes, I too remember precisely where I was when I heard the news, and for the duration of that extended weekend, when the world stood still.

As the weekend progressed, we were all collectively focused on small, black and white TV images, both live and not so instant replay. I can only speak for those my age, who missed the world's previous great tragedies, but there and then, gently guided by Walter Cronkite, we witnessed and relived an event terrible beyond imagination. And as we, the nation, re-emerged the following Tuesday, it was to a different time, a different era – the "Sixties" had begun.

Decades and Eras

I have a belief that, although we tend to mark time in decades, the actual eras do not strictly adhere to the calendar. The "Twenties" began with prohibition, and ended on a Tuesday in October of 1929. The resulting collapse and Depression began the bifurcated "Thirties," with a turning point on inauguration day of 1933. The later "Thirties" ended on December 7th, 1941.

The "Forties" are mostly thought of as the War years. The

postwar era moved slowly into and through the "Fifties" and on to November of 1963 as a single, though evolving, continuum, as we baby boomers progressed through childhood, and our parents – survivors of both the Great Depression AND the War – wanted nothing more than a good job, to raise a family in their own home, and to live in peace.

The "Sixties," beginning in tragedy and ending with another in 1970, was also a split era, with a sharp pivot in the middle. In the early period, after the Kennedy assassination, cultural changes were becoming more evident. Of course, television, and the media in general, had much to do with the transformation of a country of "regions" to a more homogeneous society, but, as always, music was the bellwether. Rock 'n roll evolved from Buddy Holly to the Beach Boys. Beat poetry gave way to the more energetic folk music and "folk rock," and several icons of the new era were emerging. The title and words of Dylan's "The Times They Are A'Changin'" were prophetic in announcing that youth was on the march:

Come mothers and fathers throughout the land
And don't criticize what you can't understand
Your sons and your daughters are beyond your command
Your old road is rapidly agin'
Please get out of the new one if you can't lend your hand
For the times they are a-changin'
                    Bob Dylan 1964

Graduation in Jeopardy – 1st Offense

For me, the earlier part of the sixties era featured my graduation from Aurora East High School in June of 1964, and my entry into the US Navy in 1965, culminating in a visit to Viet Nam in 1966.

The former event almost didn't happen though, as I managed to misbehave just enough in the closing months of the school year to possibly put the issue into doubt. Suspension may have been merely a threat; my grades, though not stellar, were adequate to see me through, and misbehaving was a far cry from causing real trouble – but I took it seriously nonetheless. Taking it seriously, however, didn't mean my behavior changed all that much; but I *was* quite concerned and consequently more careful. My two worst offenses, which seem so trivial today, were actually, even then, quite benign.

In the last semester of my last year at East High, the study hall to which I was assigned just prior to lunch was quite a long way away from the cafeteria, and a long line would form before I could get there, thus consuming a large portion of my lunch hour – actually a half hour. This seemed unfair, so to avoid standing in the long cafeteria line, I would merely find someone near the front of the line whom I knew and cut in. Problem solved.

I was plucked out of line several times and warned that this was unacceptable behavior, with the last warning threatening me with banishment from the cafeteria for the remainder of the year. I'm not sure what I *thought* would happen, but sure enough, the next time I cut in line, I was almost immediately removed and taken to see the Vice Principal, Ewald Metzger. "Ol' Ewald" was the subject of a great deal of derision and ridicule – at least among those whom I knew, or associated with – but the fact was, he had the Power. I was, indeed, banished from the cafeteria until the end of the school year, fortunately now just a few weeks away.

So, I brought my lunch and ate it, alone, in the anteroom of the teachers' lounge. The alone part was bad enough, but as the teachers passed to and from the lounge, they all managed to give me that disgusted, disappointed look, which teachers all seem to develop, and hold in reserve for those whose performance falls well below standard.

Graduation in Jeopardy – 2nd Offense

The second, and I suppose last, offense that jeopardized my impending graduation from East High was less harmful, in general, than cutting into the lunch line. But it was, in fact, a bit more serious and could indeed have gotten me suspended, just weeks before graduation. In that final semester, the last class of my day was art class – which you would think I looked forward to. Not so, for the senior art teacher to whose class I was assigned was the elderly Miss Pooley.

Close to retirement – my Uncle Ray had had her for a teacher some 20 years earlier – Miss Pooley's technique for teaching art was sometimes to snatch the brush, or pencil, or charcoal, or whatever from your hand saying, "No, like this," thus forcing you to watch while she completed most of your project for you in a sort of show and tell. Any respect I might have had for her as an art teacher vanished the first time she pulled this on me. It may have been acceptable to some in the class, but art class was one of the few where I actually looked forward to learning something, and to me represented the very definition of a participatory activity, not a lecture.

Vern, on the other hand, had signed up for "Cinema", and spent the final period setting up and showing movies to those classes requiring an audio-visual experience. When no movies were scheduled, it was to be regarded as a study hall. In fact, if no movies were scheduled, Vern would wander down to my art class and signal to me from the hall.

Miss Pooley, it turned out, was largely unaware of what actually went on in her classroom; at least as far as attendance was concerned. After she took the roll, if Vern was waiting outside, I would simply slip out one of the two doors when her back was turned, and off we went. I don't know how many times we did this, but only once did she question whether I had been in class the previous day. I, of course, professed that yes, I had been there, and others in the class – knowing full well what I had done – backed me up.

I wasn't too surprised at her question. On the previous day, as Vern and I were making our way off school grounds, we were spotted by our old nemesis, Ewald. Off we went in a flash, diving into the residential neighborhood beyond the parking lot. I think we must've been far enough away that Ewald couldn't make a positive identification, but he did hurry to his car and give chase.

It took us twice as long to get home that day as it would have had we stayed until the end of classes. We dashed across streets and hid between houses as Ewald cruised back and forth, hoping to catch us in the open. But we finally managed to break contact and get to Vern's house.

The reason I believe he did not make a conclusive identification was that the next day we were called to his office, there to be subjected to another stern warning. I'm certain that had he been able to prove it was us, our school year would've ended then and there.

But the school year ran out before my luck did, and I have a clear memory of marching – after the football field graduation ceremony – into the locker room wherein, in a most un-Vern-like fashion, my friend launched himself at me, wrapped me in a major-league hug, and exclaimed, "We made it, we made it!"

In Limbo –
Between High School and the Navy

My Left Thumb

In August of 1964, I got my first post-high school job. I was hired at All Steel Equipment Co. as a second shift "Helper" on a brake press. The No. 1 song at that time was The Beatles' "A Hard Day's Night" and I recall after a couple of days of hard nights thinking just how appropriate that was.

A very similar mechanism to the venerable punch press, a brake press is used to create bends and corners in sheet metal of gauges thick and thin. To accommodate this, the extended press bed and upper ram hold dies which come together to shape the metal sheet in between with a pressure of about 100 tons. In the primitive days of manufacturing, before the OSHA law, not only could the unshielded press be operated with a foot pedal, but if the press bed was of sufficient length, a second job could be set up to run simultaneously. It was at this second set-up that the "Helper" came into play.

So there I was, stationed at the other end of the press bed, several feet away from a skilled machine operator whose weekly pay was determined by how fast he could load the machine, press the foot pedal, and produce completed parts. My responsibility was to match his efforts by obtaining an oily sheet of metal from my own stack and to quickly place it between the open dies, then position and hold it to a backstop. All while wearing bulky leather gloves, I might add. The purpose of my doing this for eight hours was to double the machine's utilization *(translation - extra production)*. Because I was new, and working for a flat hourly rate, increased production was of little benefit to me. But as a trainee hoping to qualify for "incentive pay," I was eager to demonstrate skill, dexterity, and above all, speed.

Although I occasionally missed a cycle, I managed to perform satisfactorily for 3-1/2 nights. In the middle of the Thursday evening shift, I was starting to fall a little behind, and in my haste, I missed the backstop. Before I could stop, my left hand, to the wrist, was between the temporarily open dies. Without conscious thought, I withdrew my arm with all possible speed. My *vivid* memory of this event – my last at All Steel Equipment Co. – is of the descending upper die touching the top knuckle of my left thumb, and maintaining a sliding contact as I withdrew. I just made it. Whew! But the end of the thumb of my leather glove was neatly pinched off.

And thus, after 3-1/2 days, my first industrial experience came to an abrupt end, as I informed the machine operator, and then the department foreman that I would be seeking employment elsewhere.

Inventory at Thor Power Tool Company – A Lesson Learned

Biding my time until I reported to the Navy, my next job in September of 1964 was temporary, helping to perform the annual physical inventory at Thor Power Tool Company, where my father was a longtime employee.

This was an era when companies counted the labor cost of producing individual component parts as an important measure in the overall cost of their products, and produced large quantities of parts and partial assemblies on the notion that producing in quantity reduced the cost of each individual item, and would thus maintain warehouses and stock rooms full of such, waiting to be used.

The annual "physical inventory" was important because the government charges a tax on the value of held inventories. So, everything had to be accurately counted and recorded, a task both daunting and mind-numbingly boring for those, such as I, who were hired to do so.

I had decided that because of the nature of the work, and because the cumulative pay for any given day's work was not all that much, taking a day off was not that great a penalty. But I knew my father would certainly not approve.

My father and I rode together to and from work in the aging, but still sound, '50 Plymouth. On one of those days, we walked from the parking lot on Claim Street to, and through, the front door of the old building, as usual. As he continued on to the department in which he worked, I reversed course and walked right back to the car, having decided via a rationale which made sense to me at the time that I just wasn't going into work that day.

Instead, I drove to the West Side where a friend lived. We then picked up another friend and had a really fun day – made more so, I'm sure, by the fact that I was not in some dim warehouse, counting hundreds of small, oily, half-completed parts.

Just before 3:30 pm, I returned, re-parked the car, and waited for my dad. Getting into the car, he glanced at the dashboard noting the odometer, or the gas gauge, or something. He then

dryly commented that he hoped that I had had a good day, seeing as how I hadn't been at work. He said no more about the
matter, but it made me feel pretty low nonetheless. Lesson
learned, I never tried to fool him again.

An Electric Guitar

In the fall of 1964, Roy Orbison topped the charts yet again
with "Pretty Woman," Gale Garnett was singing in the sun-
shine, and Chad and Jeremy's "A Summer Song" lamented that
all good things must end.

This was my mood as well, as I drifted along with the vaguely
uncomfortable feeling of just waiting for what would come
next. Despite looking forward to the coming change, and the
adventure I anticipated when I entered the regular Navy, I
could not help feeling a tiny bit uneasy at the thought of leaving Aurora and all that was familiar for what, at the time,
seemed would be almost forever.

It was during this period that I met Andy, who despite being
not much older than I, seemed infinitely more worldly-wise.
Andy had his own apartment on North Avenue, and more importantly – to me anyway – played the electric guitar, and knew
others who did so, and did it quite well. Despite his age, Andy
drank a bit, and my mother, night manager at the time at
Stein's Liquor Store and Delicatessen, knew him and his downtown friends, and disliked them quite a lot. Looking back, it
must be said that deep down inside Andy *was* sort of a low-life.
My mother saw it easily. At the time, I did not. Fortunately, I
did not share in the drinking, and never met his seedier friends.

Andy quickly picked up on my interest in wanting to own,
and learn to play, a guitar; in particular the rock 'n roll electric
version. At the time, my father's nephew, George Philip – my
cousin, although he was much older – owned a music store,

then on South Lake Street. My cousin had "made his bones" with the accordion, an instrument that, with the exception of the Lawrence Welk Show, was from an earlier era. But one could go to his shop and purchase music lessons of all kinds, and of course, the instruments as well.

But Andy assured me that *he* could provide the lessons, if I only had a guitar. So off we went to see my cousin who had, among others, a used cream-colored Gibson electric guitar which might just be within my budget – if I were to forgo virtually everything else on which I might spend my meager earnings.

I made a deal for the guitar, and Andy taught me a few chords and riffs – which oddly I still remember – but, in truth, I had neither the aptitude, nor the discipline to do what needed to be done to truly learn; that is to say, pay for professional lessons and start from scratch.

In due time, I revealed to my parents that I had a guitar and was learning to play. They listened to me proudly, but amateurishly, play the few things that I had learned. They seemed pleased and were complimentary, but nonetheless, quickly sent me packing, guitar in hand, back to my cousin, where I received a stern and disappointed look, along with a full refund of my deposit.

The USS Daniel A. Joy – Reporting Aboard

Joining the Naval Reserve while still in high school set several events into place, culminating of course with actual service in the real Navy. But first, in July of 1964, I was scheduled for an abbreviated boot camp at Great Lakes Recruit Training Center. Given the nature of the shortened session required of reserves, I remain grateful for not experiencing recruit training in its entirety.

Having passed through boot training and elevated to the rank of "apprentice" – two tiny stripes – I was off in October for a two-week training cruise aboard the destroyer escort, USS Daniel A. Joy (DE 585), then in service to the reserve training fleet, and moored, almost permanently, at the foot of Randolph Street in Chicago.

When the time came, I rode a Burlington commuter train from Aurora to Chicago's Union Station, a trip I would make many times in the coming year. After walking to the lakefront, I made my way to the Randolph Street pier, and then past the WWII submarine, USS Silversides, and on to the "Joy."

World War II era destroyer escorts were not such a big deal in the grand scheme of the US Navy, as it existed in the fall of 1964, but to me it was awesome. As I walked slowly past the bow of the ship and on to the quarterdeck – located amidships – I took it all in; the large five-inch gun mount on the foredeck, the 40 mm antiaircraft guns behind and above on the next level, the bridge on yet a higher level, the towering mast, and the overall reality of it. This wasn't a Saturday night movie on TV; this was the real thing.

I stood on the pier beside the quarterdeck gangway, excited but for some reason not wanting to go aboard, until the petty officer who had the watch, standing on the deck just a few feet away from me, finally asked me just "what in the hell" I was doing.

At that, I scrambled aboard, remembering the formalities, first saluting the flag, then saluting the petty officer of the watch and requesting "permission to come aboard." This was granted, and assuming correctly that I was a reserve who knew nothing, he gave me directions. The rest of that first day passed in something of a fog as first I settled into my new environment, and then spent my time exploring.

The USS Daniel A. Joy – At Sea

The first full day of my training cruise aboard USS Daniel A. Joy started with a Monday midmorning departure from the Randolph Street pier. This two-week experience was not to be a cruise in the accepted sense, as we never actually went anywhere, but we did leave the pier several times for training exercises.

Today's mission was to depart and steam for perhaps 40 miles (roughly halfway across Lake Michigan) and back again. Being assigned to the deck force for the first couple of days gave me a once ever opportunity for which I am grateful. I can say that for a two-hour period, I stood lookout watch on the bridge wing of a US Navy destroyer "at sea."

I've always been fascinated by destroyers, as a ship type, and this experience allowed me to live out, if briefly and on a very small scale, some childhood fantasies of World War II action in the Pacific. I could, on my two-hour watch, imagine as I scanned the Lake Michigan horizon that I was watching for Japanese aircraft, or the periscopes of enemy submarines. All in all, this was great fun. Yes, I know, I was 18 years old and a "grown-up," but there was, and is, a boy within me who had a wonderful time that day.

The next day, we left the Randolph Street pier and glided smoothly to nearby, then empty, Navy Pier. There we spent most of the day docking and departing. We would cast off and leave the pier to steam perhaps a mile into the lake, only to turn back, approach the dock and tie up again. This gave the reserve officers plenty of practice at commanding the movements of the 306-foot-long ship.

This practice also extended to the line handling crews of the deck force. Being assigned temporarily to the deck, my personal responsibilities were limited to pulling on a line (rope) at the appropriate time, at the bellowed order of the Bosun's Mate who was in charge of my group.

After my brief experience as watch stander, and line handler, and otherwise general cleaning person with the deck force, I was assigned to the engineering spaces, specifically to one of the ship's two boiler rooms, where new adventures awaited.

The Boiler Room: Part One

Having served on the deck force on Monday and Tuesday, the remainder of my two-week reserve ACDUTRA (active duty for training) aboard the USS Daniel A. Joy was spent, during working hours anyway, in the ship's Forward Fireroom, otherwise known to landlubbers as the place where one of the ship's boilers was located. There was, of course, an After Fireroom somewhere behind us, but I never had occasion to go there.

Each of the two high-pressure steam turbine engines (in the Fwd and Aft Engine Rooms, naturally), which supplied power to the ship's screws (propellers, writ large), was provided steam by its complementary boiler. In addition, various ship machinery and amenities – winches, hoists, the steam whistle, the hot water for showers, etc. – were also powered or enabled by those boilers.

So, in the grand scheme of things, the two firerooms were very important places. They were also hot, a little smelly, comparatively dirty, and more than a little grim, being located, as they of course were, at the very bottom of the ship.

Each day, I would climb through a main deck scuttle – a small, round vertical hatchway just big enough for the shoulders of a slightly more than average-sized man. Once through, I would descend a narrow slippery ladder several levels down to the steel plate decking, inches above the bilge (the inside bottom of the ship's hull).

But I was happy to be there. Working on the deck force, when not doing something interesting, like arriving or departing, was simple drudgery (mostly cleaning something) for those of the lowest rank, such as myself. I was, of course, a very junior unrated enlisted man, with the additional negative of being a reserve.

But in the engineering spaces (the firerooms and the engine rooms), while still a lowly reserve, I was among my kind and there was always something requiring service or scheduled maintenance. Working in the fireroom, I was always taking something apart or putting it together, under the instruction, and watchful eyes, of the petty officers of the regular ship's crew, to whom I was assigned. I was actually learning stuff, and for the most part, having a nice time. The environment in which I did this, for two four-hour stretches each weekday, hardly mattered.

I did, however, on my very first day in the fireroom, receive an excellent lesson on the capricious nature of that environment.

The Boiler Room: Part Two

Warning: the following may be a bit disturbing to those who are squeamish about various bad things that can sometimes happen in the real world.

My first experience after being assigned to an engineering division aboard the reserve destroyer, Daniel A. Joy, is one I will never forget.

Climbing down the narrow, slippery rungs of the tiny ladder into the Forward Fireroom for the very first time, most of my attention was focused on the ladder, and trying not to slip and fall off. Thus, I was not paying much attention to what was going on at the bottom.

When I finally arrived in the cramped space between the front of the boiler and the ladder I had just descended, two of the petty officers for whom I was to work were busy removing the final bolts holding an access plate to the front of the boiler. The circular plate, though appropriately thick and somewhat large, could nonetheless be handled by the two large men. As one removed the final bolt, the other braced himself and got a firm hold, top and bottom, to support the weight until he received help relocating the plate to the deck.

Whether the weight was more than anticipated, or the pipe just below the boiler wasn't noticed – or perhaps both – as the plate was suddenly freed, it dropped far enough to contact the pipe, with one finger precisely in between. The digit was neatly lopped off at the first knuckle. The man cried out, spun around shaking his hand, and sprayed me with blood as he did so.

The victim was quickly removed to sick bay, and from there I know not. The care he received was no doubt excellent, and I'm sure that in time he recovered and returned. But I never saw him again. The lasting result to me personally was a shocking, and unforgettable lesson in shipboard possibilities, and one white-hat which I never used again.

Liberty and the Chicago Skyline

Going ashore on liberty from the reserve destroyer, Daniel A. Joy, meant an evening in the heart of Chicago, the nation's second largest city. This was interesting, but didn't really offer us very much in the way of entertainment. First, we didn't have that much time. If we went ashore, we would always leave after dinner. The Joy was, if anything, a good "feeder". Typical of smaller ships, the food was very good, plentiful, and, of course, free.

Taps was at 10 pm and we were expected, actually required, to be aboard and in our bunks at "lights out." Also, it was a time-consuming walk to the end of the pier, then up and over (in those days) Lakeshore Drive to Randolph Street and the city proper. And then back again.

In truth, in the places we could get to in that time, there really wasn't much for us anyway. The Navy uniform notwithstanding, my new friends and I, being fairly recent high school graduates, were not welcome in the bars, legally or otherwise; and on my part at least the feeling was mutual. Usually, we would get as far as Mammy's Pancake House at State and Randolph Streets and stop there. We would drink coffee and hang out, chatting when appropriate with the usually friendly waitresses.

But mostly I stayed aboard with a book, or a card game, or

bull session with the guys to fill the evening hours. But one thing I did every night before lights out was to spend a little time alone on the foredeck gazing up at the city skyline. As a youngster from a relatively small town, this was my first solo experience in Chicago, or any other large urban setting for that matter, and I truly believe it was then and there that I discovered my love for big cities.

The nighttime autumn air was getting cold, and the evening was ending, so I would be absolutely alone as I leaned back against the forward five-inch gun turret, taking it all in. The solitude, after sharing the cramped ship's spaces all day, was refreshing. And the buildings, towering over the waterfront, decorated with a billion twinkling lights, created a fairytale vision which, while commonplace to and maybe even taken for granted by *some* city dwellers, was a wonder and an epiphany to me. And I loved it! (Still do.)

In The Navy – Boston to Bangkok

In the Navy – Introduction

In the beginning of 1965, the British (music) Invasion was in full swing, and Gerry & the Pacemakers' second, and best, hit song, "Ferry Cross the Mersey," will always remind me of those first couple of months of that year, before I reported to Class A Engineman School, at Great Lakes Naval Training Center to begin my active duty service in the US Navy.

The poignancy of Gerry Marsden's ballad was enough in itself to make it a favorite, but the notion that one could love their hometown, as Marsden so obviously did, made me long to live in such a place. I didn't know much about Liverpool at the time.

Oddly, the other recollection which will always take me back to that time was going with friends to the Tivoli Theater to see Elvis starring with Ann-Margret, in what I think of as his best film, *Viva Las Vegas*. Another look at a world I had never seen.

But that was about to change. Having spent a life mostly cloistered in Aurora, I was about to begin what I can only recall as being an adventure – a learning and growing experience which would take me from Aurora, literally halfway around the world, and back again.

Class "A" Engineman School – Shaky Start

I arrived, as ordered, at the duty office of the Engineman School at Great Lakes Naval Training Center on a late winter Sunday afternoon in 1965. There to begin my active duty service in the US Navy. I was assigned a bunk, and told that I, and my classmates, would muster in front of the barracks the next morning, early. The time was not specified, but no matter, as we were all rather rudely awakened at the appropriate hour.

As we would each day, my class marched to the school building, and the first day of the 12-week session progressed without incident. When the day's classes ended, we again mustered and marched back to – and then past – the barracks to which I was assigned. Young, naïve (read stupid), and worried that I was in the wrong formation and being taken to the wrong place, in a momentary lapse I panicked, left the formation, and entered the barracks.

About 15 minutes later, a Petty Officer entered and informed me that my class, along with others, had marched to the space between barracks, there to be formally dismissed. I, however, had done a terrible thing by breaking ranks, and had thus violated a significant rule. My first day in the Navy and in trouble already. My punishment for this violation, informally administered, was restriction to the base, starting immediately, and continuing through the following weekend.

So, my classmates spent the evenings and the upcoming weekend getting familiar with "The Strip," the tawdry couple of blocks just outside the main gate in North Chicago, Illinois. Teeming with bars, locker clubs, and "gift shops," the strip's only purpose was to fleece the homesick, lonely young men seeking a diversion from the restrictive military environment on the *other* side of Sheridan Road. I, with great envy, stayed behind. The optimistic view that I decided upon was that, having started on the wrong foot, it could only get better. And, in fact, it did.

Military Life – and the "Duty"

Settling into Engineman School at Great Lakes, I quickly decided for the most part to ignore the strip, the seedy area of bars and such just outside the main gate. Being too young to frequent the bars, it soon became obvious that there was not much else there for me other than the train station, through which I traveled home to Aurora when I could. Besides, I could fill my time on weeknights, and I was close enough to go home on weekends when the opportunity presented itself.

Subject now to "The Laws of the Navy", the second thing I learned – the first being to stay in marching formation – was the concept, and reality, of "The Duty." For routine chores, military organizations are divided into sections, usually three, sometimes four, and rarely, in an emergency, two.

Duty sections rotated, so every three days, your section had the duty; thus bearing the responsibility for such things as keeping the place clean, standing watches, and in fact, all of the tedious, often trivial chores that keep things going; the sorts of things which use up your otherwise free time, every third day, and every third weekend.

This was, and is, standard practice everywhere, with Officers and Senior Petty Officers mostly required to just be there, and to be in charge, and down through the ranks to the lowly drudges, such as we students were, who got the worst jobs.

Such is military life. Actually, it's a good system for achieving personal growth and learning, otherwise known as "paying your dues." Except that every third week I found a way out of the weekend requirement.

Shot Glass in a Bottle

Another thing quickly learned at Great Lakes was that, as far as we students were concerned, the Senior Chief Petty Officer at the Engineman School, officers notwithstanding, was the one truly in charge. The Chief was a great promoter of the Navy Relief Fund, and as such, was always looking for donations and other ways of making money for his cause. One such idea was to be my weekend salvation.

We marched to the school on the second Monday to find, in the lounge area outside the office, a very large bottle filled with water. Also inside the bottle, at bottom-center, was a shot glass surrounded by a shallow, full diameter layer of dimes and quarters. Any money dropped into the bottle, we were told, would be donated to Navy Relief. The incentive to thus part with your money was that, if you could drop a dime *into* the shot glass, you would be relieved of one duty day; a quarter in the shot glass would be worth a duty weekend.

Needless to say, students were lined up to take their turn dropping coins into the glass. That is, until it quickly became clear just how difficult, perhaps nearly impossible, this was to accomplish. Quarters and dimes being worth what they were in those days, the enthusiasm quickly waned.

Like non-gamblers passing by a slot machine, who might occasionally drop a coin, knowing the probable results, and thinking, "Well maybe, just this once," students would now and then drop a coin into the bottle. It was, after all, for a good cause, and you would often see the Chief watching and smiling in an otherwise uncharacteristic way.

But it turned out that it wasn't as impossible as it seemed. The almost universally applied technique was to hold the coin upright between thumb and forefinger, then let go and hope for the best. This false hope cost many of my schoolmates many of their dimes and quarters. The coin, entering the water edge would first, would immediately shear off to the side and almost invariably land as far from the shot glass as possible.

The trick, which I discovered, was to hold the coin flat, by the edges and as you let go to give it a spin. The coin would then spiral down the center portion of the bottle, with perhaps as good as a one in three chance of landing in the glass. And so, after a bit of practice, I could get out of a duty day for as little as 30 or 40 cents.

I say duty day, because this seems to only work well with dimes. Quarters, being larger and heavier, were *much* more difficult. So, before I let it be generally known just how good I had gotten at hitting the glass, I made a proposal to the cadre of Chiefs (the school's instructors) and the Senior Chief. I argued that if a quarter was good for a weekend (two days), why couldn't three dimes (three days) also be good for a weekend.

After talking it over – I'm sure with some amusement over how many dimes I would donate – the Chief said okay, and officially amended the rules. I did not spend another weekend at the Great Lakes Naval Training Center.

Sunday Train Rides with Rocky

The only real downside of going home for the weekend from the Great Lakes Naval Training Center was the train ride back to Great Lakes on Sunday evening. This was a two-train journey, beginning with the eastbound leg on a Burlington commuter from Aurora to Chicago's Union Station, a three-block walk to the Northwestern station, and then a second train to North Chicago.

When I traveled alone, I usually left early so I could spend a few hours in Chicago's Loop, the teeming business district centered on State Street (*That Great Street*), south of the river. As

I've indicated, the bad portion of the journey was the remaining train ride north.

The Chicago Northwestern management had wisely decided to separate sailors returning from a weekend in Chicago from the other, more civilized riders. Actually, riding in the two "special" cars was hardly different than being in one of the bars from which many of the sailors had recently come. Loud, hyperactive, sometimes belligerent, and occasionally sick, they could turn a two-hour train ride into an ordeal. But, wearing the same uniform, I had no choice but to ride along.

However, as luck would have it, Vern's older brother, Ken, was engaged to a girl from Plano who was then attending nursing school in Evanston, near Northwestern University. Roxanne (Rocky) was, it turned out, taking the same trains as I, just getting off a bit sooner. We decided that it would be nice to have company on these Sunday afternoon journeys, and so we started traveling together to the North Shore.

On the first Sunday we traveled together I knew that, in uniform, I would have a bit of trouble getting onto any but the specially designated cars. But Rocky smiled sweetly at the conductor and asked if I might ride with her and the other normal people. She didn't look as if she were someone whom I had just picked up in a Chicago bar, and I also smiled and promised to behave myself, if only I didn't have to ride with those animals.

At that, the conductor smiled as well and said okay, but at Evanston I would have to rejoin the Navy; a rule which, week after week, I ignored and was never enforced. The next weekend, the same conductor recognized us and waved us aboard. So, thereafter, I spent most of the trip in pleasant company, and the remainder in quiet, and relative comfort, reading my book. All but the special cars were no smoking, but if the need overcame me as it did in those days, I could slip into the small washroom for a quick cigarette.

At North Chicago's tiny train station, I rejoined the throng as we trudged through the gathering gloom of the evening, through the main gate, and on to our respective barracks. And thus, a new week would begin.

Going East

My performance at the Navy's Class A Engineman School was typical. I settled for being an average student by not actually trying very hard. However, I left the school wearing three red stripes, which designated me a "Fireman" (Grade E-3 Enlisted), topped by an "Engineman Striker" badge.

The red stripes identified me as engineering, as opposed to deck (the generic Fireman vs. Seaman). And the striker badge indicated that, having graduated from Engineman School, I could thereafter not be arbitrarily assigned to a different engineering rating, such as electrician, or working in the boiler room.

As completion of the course drew near, with visions of World War II action and glory in my head, I requested duty aboard a destroyer. Upon graduation, I was instead detached with orders to report to the USS Tutuila, a repair ship specializing in internal combustion engines, stationed in Norfolk, Virginia.

With a short leave to consume, I spent a few days at home before departing for Norfolk via Pittsburgh, Pennsylvania. There, I would spend a few days with the Forkin family – my namesake and my father's WWII best friend, Tom, his wife, Helen, and their two boys, Skipper (Tom Jr.) and Billy.

Being quite familiar with trains at this point, I decided that the rails to Pittsburgh would get me there just fine. So, once again, into Chicago, this time to change trains at Union Station and continue heading east. My single memory of this particular train ride is of rolling out of Union Station, and bending to the south and east around the bottom of Lake Michigan. As we rounded the bight of the southern lakeshore and on through Gary, Indiana, we were in the heart of the Midwest's steel mill country – and the air was *orange*.

Since it was about 11 am, this was not the effect of a setting sun, but rather a result of the mills and other industries that polluted not only the air, but the lake and the natural wetlands of the region. We were still, at the time, several years from the awakening, and environmental turnaround, signaled by the first Earth Day. I am often amused by younger people these days who, with no memory of the not so distant past, campaign to clean up today's environment and save the earth.

I must admit that we, as a society, were quite ignorant of such things in those days and in the years prior. On one of the occasional long-weekend, mini-vacations to New York, which I was fond of taking in the late 1980s, a major news story on WCBS radio was, I recall, the locating and cleanup of landfills in what was once the marshland upon which Jersey City, New Jersey was built.

One by one, and seemingly endlessly, homes, trucking depots, factories, parks, vacant land, and an elementary school, *were identified as former landfill sites (an eventual total of 104), and were scheduled for cleanup. It seems that sometime in the mid-1950s, an inexpensive landfill material became available from two area companies. Referred to as "chromium slag," a byproduct of some manufacturing process, the stuff was, as the Jersey City officials stated at the time, a great landfill material for, in addition to filling up the wetlands, "all the rats died."*

At the end of the train ride, I was welcomed by the Forkin family. While I have no musical memory of the train trip itself, the Beach Boys' "Help Me, Rhonda" will always remind me of my visit, and of those evenings, Friday and Saturday, when my friends, Skipper and Jimmy, introduced me, briefly, to life as a teenager in Pittsburgh, Pennsylvania.

First Airplane Ride(s)

© Ed Coates Collection

When my leave ended and it was time came to re-join the Navy, the Forkin family drove me to the Pittsburgh airport. It was the spring of 1965 and, as could be done in those days, the Forkins walked me to the gate and sat with me until it was time to board. This was all a new experience for me, as this would be my very first ride on an airplane of any sort; and this would be a *jet* – perhaps a very early version of the venerable 727 – which added greatly to my excitement.

The plane left on time with me aboard, my nose pressed firmly against the window. About an hour later, I reattached my nose to the window as we began our descent and landed at National Airport in Washington DC.

I learned the procedure for changing planes, and waited patiently for the flight to Norfolk, Virginia. My second-ever flight offered what was, in those days, a somewhat more typical air travel experience. The Piedmont Airlines flight to Norfolk was on an aging DC-3, and at boarding time, I walked to and up the steps, entered the twin-engine "tail dragger" and walked uphill to my seat.

And once again we were off, and yes, my nose was to the window. My complete enjoyment of taking off and landing in aircraft large and small is still with me – although any other pleasure I might have experienced in air travel in these modern times has all but totally faded away.

The trip from National Airport – actually across the Potomac River in Arlington, Virginia – to Norfolk took longer than my previous flight, as most of the time was spent taking off and landing (good for me), as we stopped at both Richmond and Newport News before lifting off and almost immediately descending on the other side of Hampton Roads in Norfolk.

It was, by now, late on a Sunday evening and completely dark. After a bus ride to this massive naval facility, I discovered that the ship to which I was assigned was off somewhere (the Caribbean, it turned out), doing something important (????), and would not return for a few weeks.

I was directed to the "Receiving Station" – a warehouse for temporary orphans such as myself – where I stayed for a few days before being bounced around a bit while awaiting the return of my new home, the USS Tutuila (ARG-4).

The Receiving Station

The barracks-like Receiving Station was comfortable, by military standards, and quite clean. This latter fact was the logical result of the temporary residents having little to actually do. The Navy and those who have authority over those of lower rank – like me – are great believers in the notion that "idle hands are the devil's tools." So we cleaned, all day and every day, or so it seemed.

A couple of days after my arrival, I was swabbing (mopping) the deck (linoleum floor) in the lounge area when a Chief Petty Officer spotted me, and noted my "Engineman" striker badge on the "Undress" white uniform in which I toiled. He asked me if I were a qualified boat engineer. As I began to tell the Chief that I wasn't quite sure of the specific responsibilities . . . , he interrupted me, saying that if "you have that striker badge, you had damn well better be a qualified boat engineer." And so, as of that moment, I *was* a qualified boat engineer. This led to many more interesting activities than mopping the floor.

Boating on Hampton Roads

Having been plucked by the passing Chief Petty Officer from the menial tasks of keeping the Norfolk Naval Station's Receiving Center shipshape, I was now spending my days serving as a boat engineer. I still had to clean, of course, but those activities would now be at the end of each day, and limited to a single boat. This chore would also be shared by *one* of my two crewmates.

The typical Navy small boat crew was a three-man team. The Coxswain, who drove the boat, was "in charge" in all ways. He was almost certainly a boatswain's mate, and always of Petty Officer rank (comparable to a noncommissioned officer in the Army). Rounding out the crew were the "Bow Hook," an un-rated seaman of the deck force who handled lines (ropes) at the front end of the boat, and the engineer, usually a Fireman – like myself – and ideally an Engineman striker. The boat engineer not only handled lines at the aft end of the boat, but was responsible for all things related to the boat's propulsion system – mainly, the engine.

In the old days, this included its actual operation (shifting, forward or reverse, and setting the throttle) as required. This would be done in response to signals given by the Coxswain via a very loud bell, conveniently located very close to the Engineer's ear. In the more "modern" times in which I served, the engine was controlled solely by the Coxswain. So, for the rest of the crew, each journey was mostly just a boat ride.

The task that the Chief had in mind for me was as engineer on a LCVP – Landing Craft-Vehicle-Personnel in Navy parlance; the World War II era landing craft developed to deliver troops to a beach via its drop-down bow ramp (see *Saving Private Ryan*). The more peaceful pursuits in which I participated were to deliver various goods and items – some senior officer's car, perhaps – and occasionally personnel, around the Hampton Roads area, the expansive waterway formed by the confluence of several large rivers and the southern end of the Chesapeake Bay as they enter the Atlantic Ocean.

We thus spent our days plying the waters between the naval station, the D & S (Destroyer and Submarine) Piers just up the Elizabeth River, and to Newport News, across Hampton Roads on the James River. Occasionally, longer missions took us to the shipyard in Portsmouth, or to the Fleet Amphibious Base at Little Creek, Virginia, beyond the Bay Bridge near Cape Henry, where the Bay meets the Atlantic.

This turned out to be easy duty, and a great deal of fun. Alas, as I settled in, looking forward to another couple of weeks before the Tutuila returned, I and several others from the Receiving Station were suddenly assigned to temporary duty aboard the USS Vulcan, a massive repair ship docked, more or less permanently, at Pier 5. The good times were over. At least for a while.

Temporary Duty: USS Vulcan (AR5)

And guess how we spent our days aboard the USS Vulcan. That's right, we cleaned!

My Engineman Striker status counted for exactly nothing aboard the Vulcan, and although I protested that I should be assigned to the ship's Engine Repair Shop, each and every one of us was relegated as extra personnel in a deck division. Looking back, I speculate that perhaps the Receiving Station was filling up and the Vulcan simply had space, and the temporary need for extra laborers who, unlike me, had little else to do.

One of the activities in which we engaged was holystoning the expansive teak decks of the old ship. Teak decking was still common in larger ships in those days. Laid over the steel deck plating, the narrow teak boards formed a surface which provided sound footing, resistance to salt water damage, and, when clean, looked pretty spiffy. Keeping it clean, however, required two small items, and a large amount of human effort.

A holystone is a small brick of white limestone that the Navy, from its beginnings, has used to clean teak decks where they existed on ships large and small. The stone, and a swab (mop) handle used to manipulate it, were the tools. The driving force of this activity was the brute labor of a large number of sailors.

The brutes, me included in this instance, were aligned shoulder to shoulder, with the stones placed before us in a line along a single board of the wooden deck. There was a depression ground into the top of the stone into which one end of the wooden swab handle was placed, and in unison – somewhat like a Radio City chorus line – we would lean in and push the stones back and forth along the grain of the teak. A couple of lucky sailors would be assigned the easier tasks of splashing saltwater and sprinkling sand onto the deck to enhance the cleaning.

When each board was cleaned to the exacting standard of the Petty Officer in charge, a signal was given and we would index the stones one board forward, and the process would begin again, and again, and again . . . This task, on which we toiled for two full days, remains my lasting memory of the USS Vulcan – that and wishing fervently and often that I were somewhere else. The ship – to me a hulking monstrosity in most ways – did, however, have a fine looking deck.

Temporary Duty: USS Amphion (AR-13)

After six days aboard the USS Vulcan, I was reassigned yet again. This time I was happy to go, and even happier when I reported aboard the repair ship, the USS Amphion (AR-13), located not it in the main portion of the naval station, but at the D & S Piers about a mile upriver.

Aboard the Amphion, I finally got to work in a shipboard Engine Repair Shop. Located abaft (behind) the mid-portion of the ship one level below the main deck, the shop was small compared to the standard that I would later come to know. However, it was adequate for the needs of a ship not dedicated solely to the repair of internal combustion engines. The shop was a comfortable environment, the work – that which I was assigned to do – was interesting, and I immediately got along with all the personnel there. Soon thoughts, and discussions, of my requesting a transfer to stay aboard started to occur. Alas, this was not to be; the Amphion had no billet for an additional Engineman rating, and the soon to return Tutuila apparently had need for me.

A feature of the Amphion's Engine Shop was the large hatch trunk which took up a fair amount of the shop's floor space. A hatch trunk is a large opening, first in the main deck, then in decks directly below, creating a vertical passage by which items large and small may be lowered into, or lifted out of, the interior spaces using the ship's cargo crane. Under normal circumstances, hatch trunks were closed with several removable metal covers, and on the main deck, sealed by an additional watertight canvas cover as well.

One Friday, just before lunchtime, working in the Engine Shop, we heard a loud crash from somewhere below. Almost immediately a call came over the PA system for the ship's doctor to report immediately to the Metal Hold – a metal and materials storage space two decks directly below our shop.

Very soon thereafter we received a call to remove the covers from our hatch trunk, and I was ordered to help with this task. As we removed the covers – and covers were removed on the deck immediately below – a terrible scene presented itself.

A few days prior, in the Metal Hold, several large thick metal plates used for patching the sides or the decks of ships, had been delivered and temporarily leaned against one of the ships frame members and secured with a large C-clamp. On this day, a sailor had removed the clamp in preparation for properly stowing the plates. When he did so, the plates toppled, trapping him beneath.

It was this scene, and the futile attempts by the ship's doctor to revive the sailor, which met my eyes; a site I will never forget. It was a mournful weekend aboard the Amphion, and appropriately rainy and grim. I recall being awakened the next morning to a memorial message on the PA. For me, the petty annoyances of recent weeks – the loss of my boat engineer job, holystoning the decks of the Vulcan, not being able to stay with my new friends aboard the Amphion – were put into stark perspective. Before going to breakfast that Saturday morning, I stood along an outside passageway and stared out at the gloomy, rain-swept Elizabeth River and felt sad, and alone, and *very* homesick.

USS Tutuila – At Last

After an all too short stay aboard the USS Amphion, the repair ship USS Tutuila (Too Too Wee' La) returned to Norfolk and tied up at its customary spot. I was detached and left the Amphion with a heavy heart; due not only to the recent tragedy, but because I was leaving what had quickly become an otherwise happy home. I had fit in nicely in the Amphion's Engine Shop, and had made new friends. I also liked that the ship was located at the D & S Piers which were separated, just a bit, from the main portion of the naval station.

I was fond of the destroyer, as a ship type, and had originally, unsuccessfully, requested assignment to one of these "grey-hounds of the fleet." While this was not to be, at least aboard the Amphion I was surrounded by destroyers, and could at least feel that I was somehow a part of it all.

So once again, for good or bad, I ventured forth into the unknown. I transported myself, and all of my stuff, to my new destination; this time the repair ship USS Tutuila (ARG-4), located at Pier 2 of the sprawling main complex of the naval station.

Also tied up just then at Pier 2, across from the Tutuila, was the USS Long Beach (CGN-9), a guided missile cruiser with the distinction of being, at the time, one of only three surface ships with nuclear power; the others being the USS Bainbridge (DLGN-25), and the famous aircraft carrier, the USS Enterprise (CVN-65) – successor to the even more famous USS Enterprise (CA-6), of WWII fame.

Also on Pier 2, at the time of my arrival, was a sharp looking Marine detachment from the Long Beach going through close order drills. It was through this altogether impressive example of the real Navy that I walked, with all my stuff, to my new home; an ancient – but nonetheless shipshape – member of Service Fleet, Atlantic.

The "Toot" was the last remaining repair ship dedicated almost exclusively to the service and repair of diesel engines, which the Navy employs in great numbers. From small boat engines, to generators, to the main propulsion of small ships, diesel engines are, literally, everywhere, and the Tutuila's large I.C.E. (Internal Combustion Engine) Shop was kept quite busy.

In the US Navy, ships are named by type, and each type for particular things (i.e., battleships were named after US states, aircraft carriers – with exceptions – were in those days named after battles [or for *very* important persons], destroyers for war heroes, and submarines for fish and other sea creatures, and so forth).

Ships of the ARG (Auxiliary Repair, Engine) class to which the Tutuila belonged were named for islands which were, or had been, owned by the United States. Tutuila is, in fact, the principal island of American Samoa, on which its capital, Pago Pago, is located. So our old repair ship did have an exotic, if somewhat unusual, name.

Life and Work Aboard the "Toot"

Upon reporting aboard the USS Tutuila, I was assigned, as expected, to the I.C.E. Shop. As the Tutuila was by designation a specialist in diesel engine repair, this was, to those of Engineman rating at least, the hub of the ship's activities.

I was assigned to Repair Division One and was given a quick tour of the ship. I was assigned a rack (bed) which consisted of a tube frame, slightly larger than myself, with canvas stiffly lashed in the middle, upon which lay a thin mattress. The racks – mine and those of my 34 roommates – were attached via hinges and small chains to side walls, or to rows of poles, with six racks on each side. Each morning, all racks were triced (folded up and secured) thus providing space for daytime activities.

The berthing spaces for repair divisions (and engineering divisions) were, by a long-standing naval tradition, located in the aft portion of the ship. This comes, I'm sure, from the fact that, in the days of sail, there *were* no engineering personnel, and the entire crew – officers excepted – slept in the forward part of the ship. When the steam engine was invented, and quickly adapted for naval propulsion, there was a sudden need to accommodate those bothersome grease monkeys. It was at that point, I'm guessing, that some deck officer decided to "put 'em in the back somewhere," and so it has been ever since. Deck divisions, and generally any enlisted who were *not* engineers, lived in the forward part of the ship, far from the constant thrashing and thumping of the ship's propeller when at sea.

The personnel working in the I.C.E. Shop were divided into three groups. This organization was not strictly adhered to but –

emergency jobs or special needs notwithstanding – the group to which you were assigned was your primary job.

One group (the elites) was dedicated to the repair and/or re-building of fuel injectors for various diesel engines – from small to very, very large. This group had their own compartment (room) within the larger shop (a space often used – after hours – as our poker parlor, as well).

The second, occasionally supplemented, group was tasked with large engine repair. This almost always took place aboard other ships, which had come to us to solve and fix their propulsion or generator problems.

The third, and largest, group – to which I was assigned – focused on small boat engines, primarily the four-cylinder Gray Marine diesel, and the ubiquitous six cylinder, supercharged GM 6-71*, the real workhorse of the small-boat Navy. The job of this third group was mostly day-to-day routine, as we maintained a large rack full of freshly overhauled engines from which we could dispense an immediate replacement when given an engine requiring a rebuild. This service made us very popular with ships having to adhere to sometimes very tight movement schedules.

And so I settled into the daily routine, only occasionally interrupted by voyages to the Caribbean, or once to Rhode Island, or to the shipyard in Portsmouth, Virginia, or finally, through the Panama Canal and beyond.

The Norfolk YMCA

Outside Gate 2 of the sprawling Norfolk Naval Station, on Admiral Taussig Boulevard, there was a "strip"; much like the

---

* *Some months later, on the other side of the world, we would largely focus on the V12-71s of the Swift Boats, and the V6-53s of the River Patrol Boats (PBRs).*

one outside the Great Lakes Naval Training Center. I would
learn that every military facility has such an area "just beyond
the wall" and Norfolk, being a huge naval facility and also Atlantic Fleet headquarters, of course had *its* version.

The Norfolk strip had its bars and gift shops, of course, but
the only business with which I concerned myself was with one
of the "locker clubs." Enlisted sailors, at that time, were required to wear the uniform both on the base, and when leaving
and returning. A locker club, as the name might suggest, was a
large, usually second-floor, room filled with lockers which could
be rented for a monthly fee, and where sailors could keep their
civilian clothes.

This provided us with a place outside of the gates to change,
thus allowing us to, hopefully, present ourselves to the Norfolk
citizenry (well, the girls anyway) as normal people – although
I'm sure we didn't fool anyone. Conveniently, there were also a
few sinks and showers. The genius of locker clubs as business
establishments was that they were almost universally located
above a men's clothing store – which, of course, offered easy
payment plans to military personnel.

I recall the Norfolk strip as being not quite as large as the one
at Great Lakes; probably for the simple reason that, unlike
North Chicago in Illinois, in Norfolk there was actually somewhere else to go. The area outside Gate 2 also included a bus
stop, and for a dime, a simple bus ride took you to downtown
Norfolk, which offered many more opportunities for lonely
young sailors to be exploited.

One of the (few) non-exploitative features, near the end of
the bus route in downtown Norfolk, was the YMCA, which
organized and hosted activities for the many, many young sailors (and marines, and others – but mostly sailors) who filled the
downtown area on evenings and weekends.

Principal among these events were dances. These were much

like the dances at the "Y" back home in Aurora, but here everyone was a bit older, and no one knew anyone else. Here, everyone was a stranger, and the competition to dance, or to just talk with the local Virginia girls who volunteered to entertain the lonesome boys, could sometimes be overwhelming. But it was occasionally worth the effort.

The Birds

Among its entertainment, the downtown Norfolk YMCA had a room that served as a small theater where they played movies, which were free to anyone with a military ID card, and which filled many a lonely hour. It was here that I saw a lot of Frankie and Annette and various beach parties, as well as many other first-run films.

One Saturday evening, I stopped into the "Y" to see what was happening – just in time to see the movie *The Birds*. And see it I did. I will admit that by the time the film ended, it had thoroughly scared the hell out of me.

The next day, on board the ship, as several of us were hanging about in the Engine Repair Shop – our weekday workspace and afterhours lounge – the ranking member of the group decided it was time to tidy the place up a bit. When we had done this, one of the Petty Officers told me to empty the wastebasket into the dumpster on the pier to which the ship was moored. I didn't have the duty, but it was a simple request, and not the sort of thing that one refused when requested by a Petty Officer whom, on other days, you worked for.

So off I went, up the ladder (stairs), through the mess decks (dining hall), on to the main deck (outside) to the quarterdeck (entranceway), down the gangway (ramp), and onto the pier. The dumpster was quite large, so a set of steps and a small platform had been erected to get you high enough to actually deposit your trash into the receptacle. Without looking, I dumped the contents of my wastebasket into the dumpster, and also onto a seagull that happened to be inside just then searching for its lunch.

The startled gull was huge; there was barely room inside the dumpster for its wingspan as it started to fly up, and out, and past a very startled me still staring down into the trash. Having watched the movie *The Birds* no more than 16 hours prior, and perhaps even having had a minor nightmare featuring vicious avian creatures, I had the hell scared out of me once again. I turned and scurried back to the gangway, up onto the ship, and safely inside where I'm sure I stayed for the rest of the day.

Bus Rides Back to the Naval Base

Not unlike the previously mentioned Sunday night train rides to Great Lakes, the bus ride at the end of a long night in downtown Norfolk was an ordeal as well – shorter yes, but actually worse.

The focal point of an evening's activities in Norfolk – a city which loves the Navy, but often disdains the sailor – was Granby Street, and it was there, in a one-block "turnaround" that the bus *from* the naval base became the bus *to* the naval base. As the bus turned onto Granby Street, it stopped to pick up passengers and, if space was available, stopped again, one block later, to take on more before turning to begin its trundling journey back to Gate 2.

It was at these two stops that, at peak times – that is to say around the time the bars closed – it seemed that every sailor on every ship in Norfolk would gather to wait for the bus. During this "rush hour," usually two buses were run together to accommodate the volume. This still didn't assure a seat, or even of getting on a bus at all.

The secret to getting an actual seat on the bus turned out to be quite simple, however. I would just walk a block to the stop just prior to Granby Street. There I would board a virtually empty bus and choose the seat I wanted. Once seated, I braced myself for the ride; but at least I was off my feet, and next to a window at that.

Once the bus got rolling, there was, as was proven, always additional space to be found. This was dramatically demonstrated one night when, halfway to the base, a young sailor standing within the crush of the bus's center aisle, suddenly groaned, opened his mouth, and tipped his head forward. There was, instantly, a relatively large clearing in front of the sailor. Someone, as a courtesy to the bus company maintenance crew, I suppose, removed the sailor's white-hat and placed it on the floor, into which the boy's liquid entertainment of the evening was neatly deposited. Yuck.

Turfing at Virginia Beach

In the mid-1960s, Virginia Beach was not the sprawling summer tourist/beach vacation destination that it is today. Rather, it was a sleepy beach community whose noteworthy features were its proximity to Norfolk, the numerous military facilities, and its location as the southern terminus of the Chesapeake Bay Bridge. And, oh yes, it had a pretty terrific beach.

It was to Virginia Beach that some of the Tutuila's crew brought their turf boards, and on a Saturday, soon after reporting aboard the "Toot," I was asked to join the group and go turfing. So I tagged along, and had the opportunity to give it a try. I did, and I liked it. Soon, I was in the ship's Carpenter Shop, after hours, fabricating a board of my own.

A turf board was easily crafted from a piece of plywood perhaps 2-½ feet long, and almost as wide, with broadly rounded corners and smoothly beveled edges. The boards would be sanded, and smoothly varnished, sometimes with a name or logo captured below its top surface.

Operating the thing was simple; I would stand at the water line and wait for a wave to reach its acme. Then, as the water began to recede, slowly moving seaward, I would run parallel to the ocean, throw down my board, and jump on. That's when the fun started, as I would ride the shallow sheet of water until one of several things happened.

The most benign result would be, as the board began to lose speed – and/or water to support it – was that I would simply step off and wait for the next wave. The worst would occur if I got my weight a bit too far forward, pushing the front edge of the board into the sand, thus causing it to come to an immediate stop. I, however, would continue moving rapidly forward, tumbling onto the flat, dense, wet sand, which felt at that moment like so much concrete.

The tumbling part notwithstanding, this was great fun. I, and others, would spend a fair number of weekend afternoons turfing, and enjoying the beach and the surrounding community. And when the Tutuila visited San Juan, Puerto Rico, which had a similar beach, we would have our boards.

Alas, before the next summer rolled around, we will have departed Norfolk for good, and I would never again have the chance to "Ride the Wild Turf."

Dry Dock

After returning from a brief support role in the failed civil war in the Dominican Republic, the "Toot" was scheduled for an overhaul at the Portsmouth Naval Shipyard, just up the Elizabeth River and across from the "other end" of Norfolk. So, one mid-summer morning, we got underway from Pier 2 and proceeded to the shipyard.

Steaming up-river was very different from an ocean voyage, and it was fun to hang around on the main deck, watching the Virginia riverbank slip by while listening to Sonny and Cher sing "I Got You Babe" on someone's transistor radio.

Arriving at the shipyard, we were nudged into a dry dock large enough to accommodate an aircraft carrier. The ship was carefully positioned, water was pumped out, and the ship settled onto a large number of enormous wooden blocks, whereupon the refit period began. And there we stayed for the remainder of the summer and into the autumn of 1965 as the crew assisted shipyard workers, and vice versa, to repair, refurbish, and upgrade the ship's machinery, equipment, and the ship itself.

What we did not know, at the time, was that much of the upgrade was in preparation for a trans-Pacific voyage to, and service in, the Republic of Viet Nam, which was experiencing a bit of turmoil at the time.

In Trouble Again – The Metal Hold

I don't recall precisely what I did, but while we were in the shipyard at Portsmouth, I was restricted to the ship for two weeks. Like my earlier misstep at Engineman School, this punishment was administered informally – this time by the Senior Chief of my division. It also included temporary banishment to the ship's "Metal Hold" for a period which was to last until such time as they were no longer mad at me.

The Metal Hold was a grim environment located beneath the cargo openings in the main deck, and several interior decks; in other words, at the bottom of the ship. It was here that all of the raw materials, the metals at least, were stored prior to use in the various repair shops whose existence were the reason for the ship's being.

It was here that I toiled, taking deliveries of and stowing various stocks of metal: plates and bars and pipes, primarily. When not taking deliveries, we were filling requests from the repair divisions, gathering the various materials, and sending them back out. It was tedious, sometimes difficult work, which occasionally required brute strength, and was potentially dangerous.

I remembered well my experience while working in the Engine Shop of the USS Amphion, and the sight of the boy who had made a simple mistake and ended up under several large, half-inch thick, steel plates. That image remained with me – and still does when I think of it – so I was very careful.

At the end of two weeks, while I remained in the Metal Hold for just a bit longer, my restriction was lifted and I was free to leave the ship on liberty. At the end of the workday, and after a quick shower, that's precisely what I did, probably making a beeline for Harry's Whitehorse Tavern, our favorite hangout in Portsmouth.

One of the few things I remember of that evening was walking, very late at night, in the general direction of the shipyard gate, and of Tom Bustos – the First Class Petty Officer who ran the Fuel Injector Repair Shop within our Engine Shop – stopping his car to offer me a ride back to the ship. I also remember being grateful; not only for the ride, but for the fact that without it, I'm not sure I would've found the ship, which would, of course, have led to further difficulties.

The next morning, I somehow managed to report on time for the day's work in the Metal Hold, and gamely tried to keep up with the day's responsibilities. As the day slowly progressed, I'm sure the Petty Officer who ran the place sometimes looked the other way only because, although my performance that day was very much sub-par, I didn't stop trying (another of life's lessons, I think).

The next morning, I arrived in the Metal Hold a few minutes early. I was alone and took the opportunity to lie back on a stack of metal plates, and to close my eyes briefly while I let my breakfast settle in. My boss walked in, took one look and exclaimed, "Oh no! Not again." At that I jumped up, assured him that I was fine, and was not only ready for the day's activities, but eagerly looking forward to them. I had a strong sense of what I had gotten away with the day before, and was grateful.

A couple of days later, my penance was finally over and I returned to the Engine Shop. Again, I don't precisely remember what it was that I had done, but I know I never did it again.

Harry's Whitehorse Tavern – Portsmouth, Virginia

While in the shipyard for overhaul at Portsmouth, the focus of our time ashore shifted. We could, and often did, go to downtown Norfolk, of course, for the 10-cent bus fare (each way), via the tunnel under the Elizabeth River to the Norfolk terminus located – where else – on Granby Street.

I recall very late one evening – on the day my restriction to the ship was lifted – riding the tunnel bus back to Portsmouth with my head hanging out the window – for reasons upon which I will not elaborate – with the tunnel wall whizzing by inches away.

But our favorite hangout that late summer and autumn was a place called Harry's Whitehorse Tavern, on Portsmouth's main avenue. I don't know exactly what made it so popular, for it was typical of such establishments. On a corner, with both a front and a side door, it boasted a bar and some tables, a jukebox, and all the 3.2 beer or inexpensive (read "cheap") wine which you would care to purchase (in my case, not all that much, but . . .).

My after-the-fact uncertainty as to why I liked the place so much at the time is compounded by the facts that I hated 3.2 beer, the wine was dreadful, and the "aroma" of the men's room could knock you down. But all of my friends went there, the management and the female patrons were friendly to sailors, and the jukebox had a good selection – although to this day I can't hear "Woolly Bully" or "Shotgun" without thinking of my times there.

Sea Trials, Guantánamo Bay Cuba

After a period of overhaul and refit in the shipyard at Portsmouth, the USS Tutuila returned quite briefly to Pier 2 before departing for Guantánamo Bay, Cuba to undergo "sea trials." This was, and still is I would suppose, the Navy's way of ensuring that the old ship was not only as good as new, but hopefully better.

The trials, which actually began on our way to the Caribbean, and continued in the startlingly blue waters south of Guantánamo, were an exhaustive series of tests and exercises – including what could laughingly be called "speed runs," during which the old liberty hull would "air it out" at 11 knots.

All of this mechanical huffing and puffing proved that all was well. This was to be expected, as both the shipyard personnel, and the Navy were (are) quite good at taking care of their assets. But a measure of any ship's seaworthiness also includes a sharp, well-trained crew. This, of course, meant many, many drills, which honed the crew's skills, and which were of course graded by the Gitmo evaluators.

My small part in all of this was as a member of one of several "damage control" repair crews. For General Quarters (Battle Stations), or for any ship's emergency, the repair crews would gather below decks, in designated areas, and wait for action. The Navy had learned well, and remembered, the lessons of WWII, and so a large portion of the training – and grading – was oriented toward firefighting. My job was to carry, and deploy as required, the "Access Kit," a bulky canvas bag containing a large pry bar and sledgehammer, and other assorted tools which I might use for the firefighting/repair crews to gain access to compartments involved in fire, calamity, or any other problem.

Short of a real emergency, of course, *my* "problem" was carrying, when called upon, the heavy, clumsy bag, at a run, through the cramped spaces, but we all performed to a satisfactory level. The ship was awarded a Navy "E" for excellence – the Navy's very visible way of saying "Well Done" – which would be prominently displayed thereafter, for all the world to see on the ship's bridge structure This greatly pleased the Captain, which made the officers happy, which in turn made life a bit easier on all the rest of us.

Despite the grueling schedule, we *were* given time off in the evenings – and once, for a whole day, during which the Captain hosted a "Beer and Barbeque" party for the crew on a palm-ringed bluff overlooking the sea. On every other day, we would get underway early in the morning for trials and drills, and return in the later afternoon. When "In Port" we would anchor in our designated spot. The Gitmo piers, such as they were, were reserved for more important vessels than ours, so for liberty we rode the ship's boat to the landing. From there, we would walk to the nearby Enlisted Men's Club or to such other recreations as there were.

After all of the effort and the trials successfully completed, we weighed anchor for the last time at Guantánamo Bay and steamed eastward to our reward – a visit to one of our favorite places.

A Visit to Puerto Rico

After completing our post-refit sea trials and departing from Guantánamo Bay, Cuba, our reward for a job well done was a visit to what was then the Tutuila's favorite liberty port – San Juan, Puerto Rico.

Upon arrival, and after we were properly secured to the pier and all formalities met, liberty commenced. Given that this was our sole purpose for being there, and there was no regular "ship's work" – that is to say, no repairs – to be performed, time ashore for those not burdened with the duty were day-and-evening long events for two of every three days we were there. Or, for as long as the money lasted anyway.

Most of the crew, for most of the time, swarmed San Juan's "Old City," which catered to the Navy in the way it now serves Caribbean cruise ships. The principal difference being that the seedy bars of 1965 far outnumbered the tourist shops and chic restaurants which are found in today's San Juan.

The old city of San Juan, which dates back to the days of the Spanish explorers, lies between the fortress of San Cristobal and the del Morro Castle, which guards the entrance to the bay and harbor. The many bars and other entertainments notwithstanding, this place – with its history of pirates and conquistadores – was fascinating to explore, and simple sightseeing was, in and of itself, an interesting and, importantly, inexpensive activity

However, sometimes we would venture further, and into the new city we would go – the portion of San Juan which occupies the peninsula bounded by the northern shoreline and the bay. Here, to the west of the harbor, the castles, and the old city was a splendid beach – similar in contour to the broad, hard, flat sands of Virginia Beach – to which we would bring our "turf boards." This also was, and is, an area occupied by the city's more affluent residents, and which also featured many grand

and luxurious beachfront hotels, in front of which we would stroll, along Avenida Ashford, imagining what wonders there might be, just on the other side of the looking glass.

Of all the big hotels, I was most captivated by the San Geronimo Hilton, occupying what was, in days past, the site of a lesser fortress. I recall gazing at the grand edifice, promising myself that I would – on some unimaginably far-off day – return as a guest (something I did, some 40 years later, thanks to American Airlines, and *a lot* of Hilton Honors points).

Old San Juan – Luna Street

Of my visits to San Juan aboard the USS Tutuila, I seem to recall the first most vividly. A shipmate and I went ashore on our first day, seeking "excitement, adventure, and really wild things." To get the afternoon started, we bought a bottle of the local rum and a one-liter bottle of, God help me, 7-Up. We then found a cab and asked the driver to take us to a nice beach.

Just east of the big hotels, along the northern shoreline, was a broad beach, visited in those days mostly by the local population. There we enjoyed the surf, and the freedom, and the exotic setting, while consuming an adequate amount of our drinks.

But, rum and 7-Up notwithstanding, the surf and the setting soon got boring. So, we walked around a bit, taking in the sights and, for us, the newness of it all. Finally, we hailed another cab to take us to the old city, specifically Luna Street, where we expected to, and did, make contact with others of Tutuila's crew.

There we explored the city of conquerors, and pirates, and colonials, stopping occasionally to patronize the local businesses (that is to say, the bars), taking advantage of the fact that there was no Puerto Rican statute requiring us to be 21 years old to do so. We eventually made our way to what many thought to be the best bar in town.

Holding court at his favorite San Juan bar was our division officer, Mr. Robertson, a grizzled Chief Warrant Officer who, scuttlebutt (rumor) had it, was a survivor of the Bataan death march, and whom we both feared and respected. So we were on our best behavior.

This, of course, didn't mean no fun; just don't get too drunk and make a fool of yourself, and spoil someone else's good time – particularly that of the boss. Good advice, and mostly followed. When not followed, there would be consequences back aboard the ship. So, while I managed to have a good time, all in all, my "P's and Q's" were carefully watched. I had once been on "Robbie's" bad list, thank you, and wanted no more of it.

Mess Cooking

Serving aboard the USS Tutuila in the fall of 1965, I was assigned to temporary duty as a "Mess Cook." This was something every enlisted man below the rank of Petty Officer faced as a matter of course. Mess cooks were the grunt labor needed to assist the cooks in every menial, miserable task associated with preparing and serving three meals every day to an entire ship's crew. Equally important was the task of cleaning up after three meals a day – an activity in which the lordly cooks took no part. The assignment was for a standard duration of three months. One of the worst positions, I had determined, was Scullery Duty, one step below the dishwashers and requiring the cleaning of all pots and pans. The plum job, of which no one seemed to know before the fact, and thus could not be hoped for, was working for the "Jack of the Dust."

This was the traditional name for the most senior cook, and assistant to the Chief Petty Officer who was in charge. The Jack of the Dust planned menus, ordered and kept track of stores, and indicated what food stuffs were to be taken from stores by the mess cooks for each meal. In fact, he ran the place, and working for him was a cushy job – really just a glorified warehouse clerk with regular hours. Somehow, this was the job to which I was assigned. No getting up at 4:30 am and working well past the dinner hour for me, at least not until the weekend before Thanksgiving of 1965.

I was told early on Friday that another fellow and I would be assigned to the Scullery for the weekend. I don't remember the exact reason, but there was a personnel shortage for those two days and we were needed. Needless to say, I was furious. I still marvel at the audacity of arguing, vehemently, with a First Class Petty Officer AND a Chief, about how unfair it was, and so on. Luckily for me, the Jack of the Dust liked me and the Chief was a mild sort. Not so mild, however, that my arguments had any effect. I was stuck with two days in the Scullery.

I think I learned a valuable life lesson that weekend, and in the week that followed. I resigned myself to my fate, and made sure I was awakened at 4:30 am on Saturday morning, and that I showed up in the galley on time. As the day progressed, and breakfast, lunch, and dinner pots and pans came to me, I stoically bent to the task and did my work. I did the same the next day and the ordeal was over. The other guy didn't argue about the assignment, but showed up late both days and noticeably slacked off at every opportunity.

The next day, my boss told me he had gotten good reports about me and that I had done a good job. On Tuesday I was given the task of painting one of the smaller stores compartments, a soft job, and was told that when the job was completed on Wednesday afternoon, I could leave the ship with a four-day pass for the Thanksgiving weekend, something absolutely unheard of for a mess cook.

An Overnight Bus Ride

I left the Tutuila mid-afternoon on Thanksgiving Eve, bound for the Greyhound Bus station in Norfolk, and ultimately for Pittsburgh, PA. I would be spending Thanksgiving with our old family friends, the Forkins.

The bus ride was an evening and overnight event, with a change of busses in Washington, DC. Arrival in Pittsburgh was scheduled to be sometime around 8 am Thanksgiving Day. The layover in DC was long enough, and boring enough, that I left the station for a late night walk in our capitol city, in which I had never been. As I walked along a dark quiet avenue, I turned a corner and was suddenly confronted with a spectacular view of the brightly lit Capitol building and dome – a most famous and compelling sight, and I was awestruck. Also, homesickness being a minor, but constant nag, I was sad that I was not sharing the experience with my family and/or friends.

I didn't wander much further, as the midnight hour was approaching and the departure time for my bus to Pittsburg was drawing near. But I vowed to return and explore the capital city at length at a later time, something I did prior to my sojourn in Viet Nam, and several times after, for the historical aspect of the city is, or should be, magical to every American.

Unlike Philadelphia, which I maintain is an absolute must visit for every American. However, having visited the many, very important, historical sites which that city holds, one is relieved of the need to ever go there again.

And so, on to Pittsburgh. Too young to fully grasp the experience at the time, I am reminded in more recent years of that midnight-to-dawn bus ride when I hear the bridge lyric from the Paul Simon song, "Ace in the Hole":

Riding on this rolling bus, beneath a stony sky,
With a slow moon rising, and the smokestacks drifting by,
In the hour when the heart is weakest and the memory is strong,
When time has stopped and the bus just rolls along
                                    Paul Simon 1979

Even traveling to visit old friends, to a youngster far from home, the experience was remarkably powerful.

The Boiler Room – Redux

My rotation working as a, sort of, mess cook ended and I returned to the daily routine of working in the Engine Shop where December passed without incident. A short leave allowed me to return home for Christmas of '65. I was a seasoned traveler now; I flew both ways. Upon returning to the "Toot," I found that, due to a temporary personnel shortage in Engineering, several of the junior personnel from the Repair Divisions, including me, were assigned to stand watches on duty days in the ship's boiler room.

Located in the very bottom, center of the ship, a four-hour In-Port watch in the boiler room was simple, and actually quite boring – especially alone on late-night or early morning watches. The primary responsibility involved little more than paying attention to conditions and, when necessary, turning the appropriate valve to either add or remove water to maintain a more or less precise level in the boiler's feed water tank; a task which amazingly was beyond the capabilities of one of my fellow temporary watch standers.

One night, he allowed the water level to go too low, for too long, and finally "corrected" his error by removing yet more water. The resulting action of the burners on the lower part of the boiler – without the heat-absorbing effect of water turning into steam – ultimately caused extensive damage. This event, and its aftermath, made me very glad that, boredom notwithstanding, I paid attention on my watches.

Newport, Fall River, and a Battleship

© 1967 Bill Rogerson

In January of 1966, while the Beatles were "Working It Out" and "Day Tripping," and Len Barry was musically counting "1-2-3," we left Pier 2 in Norfolk and the Tutuila steamed up the stormy Atlantic coast to Newport, Rhode Island, there to service a squadron of destroyers. Newport was, I'm sure, a welcome respite for the destroyer sailors after an extended period with NATO's anti-submarine force in the wintry North Atlantic, and an interesting diversion for us. And while we did a lot of work in that four-week period, we had a lot of fun, as well.

Mostly surrounded by the waters of Narragansett Bay, Newport is quite cold in the winter. A foggy 10° Fahrenheit, I discovered, can be very much more uncomfortable than a dry, crisp 0° or below on the prairies of Illinois. But we made do. A lot of shore-leave time, for me and my friends at least, was spent at and around a place called Kukla's Kitchen, a small café which brought home to me the reality of the term "greasy spoon" restaurant. Cuisine notwithstanding, it was a pretty good hangout with, most importantly, friendly waitresses.

One weekend, a friend and I took a day trip, courtesy of a Greyhound bus, to Fall River, Massachusetts, whose most famous resident remains Lizzie Borden. Going there, I recalled the 19th century rhyme which memorialized her and fixed her place in the nation's history:

Lizzie Borden took an ax, and gave her mother forty whacks
And when she saw what she had done, she gave her father
forty-one.

                                                    Anonymous

We chose Fall River as a destination because it was different, sounded interesting, and it was something to do. So on a snowy Saturday, we set off from Newport on a one-hour bus ride to visit what turned out to be a dreary New England industrial city on the Taunton River. In fact, the only thing of any interest in Fall River was the World War II battleship, USS Massachusetts, tied to a lonely pier next to the I-195 bridge. What would later become the centerpiece of a large museum called "Battleship Cove," the ship was closed and silent in the falling snow.

Still, it was a sight to behold, looming over the dock; its fighting top level with the high bridge span beside which it was moored. Up until that point, the largest ship I had seen – other than aircraft carriers, which are quite different – was the heavy cruiser, the USS Newport News, which was pretty big. But this obsolete battleship was massively larger, and impressive, even in this drab and remote setting. In later years, I would visit Battle-ship Cove and tour the Massachusetts, as well as her sister ship, the USS Alabama in Mobile, and the still larger USS New Jersey in Trenton and the USS Iowa in San Pedro, California. But this first glimpse of the ultimate of 20th century naval surface power was unforgettable.

A Weekend in Boston

During the USS Tutuila's month in Newport, a shipmate and I decided to see Boston, its historic sites, and any other entertainment that we might encounter. So, with liberty passes in hand, we again rode the Greyhound north, this time bound for the red brick city of Boston.

Despite the cold weather, and a couple of traumatic events, we did see the sights and managed to have a pretty good time. We saw the old North Church and the statue of Paul Revere in the small park across the way. We boarded and toured "Old Ironsides" in the midst of the then still active Boston Navy Yard. While in the Charlestown section, we visited the site of the Battle of Bunker Hill, climbing to the top of what is actually Breed's Hill, and then to the top of its monument to the fierce Revolutionary War battle which was fought here ("Don't fire until you see the whites of their eyes"). In the tall spire's narrow observation space, we enjoyed a spectacular, if quite frigid, view of Boston and the Charles River.

At some point on Saturday afternoon, as we wandered lost through the meandering ex-cow paths which are the streets of central Boston, we found ourselves in an area referred to as the "Combat Zone." Based on reputation alone, this was not a part of town we would've chosen to visit, but being world-weary 19-year-old sailors we pressed on, undaunted by the sordid surroundings. It was just then, however that the first major event of the day took place as the boiler in the basement of a nearby hotel quite dramatically exploded.

I don't believe anyone was really injured, and after the initial shock, it was quite exciting as police and fire units converged from all directions, taking charge, keeping back crowds of gawkers – including us – and somehow dealing with a number of dazed hotel guests and staff who seemed to be just wandering about. We stayed and rubber-necked some more, and were entertained by the action until it dawned on us that we needed to get about finding a place to stay for the night. The choice we made led to the second event of the day (or night actually).

After a brief search, we decided to spend our night in a modest (meaning cheap) lodging called "The Beacon Chambers." I had heard of Beacon Street and, of course, Beacon Hill in Boston and assumed that this meant we were in an okay part of town; an assumption which proved to be almost, if not entirely, untrue.

A Weekend in Boston: The Beacon Chambers Hotel

The accommodation upon which we settled for our night in Boston was the typical choice for a couple of sailors in a strange city and on an extremely limited budget. The Beacon Chambers was inexpensive and adequate. What this meant in practical terms was that it was very cheap, but not a complete hovel. Another feature, not surprising in retrospect, was that it proved to be somewhat dangerous.

After checking in, we went back out for the evening, returning and settling in at about 11 pm (it had been a long day). We quickly became aware of an ongoing argument between two "guests" in the room across the hall. Rather than an argument, or confrontation, it was really more of a continuing series of bellowed beratements, occasionally answered by groveling supplication.

Before turning in, I made the trip down the hall to the communal washroom, and on my way back, I knocked on the door across the hall – which was standing open by about six inches. As I did so, I called out, "Hey, you think you could keep it down?" The first thing I heard in response was a groveling voice, pleading, "No, please don't." At the same time, through the gap in the door, I saw a portion of a rather large man turning toward the door. The motion exposed his arm to view, and in his hand, I saw what was more than a rather large knife.

I immediately did the logical thing, spinning and scurrying into our room, slamming and locking the door. Very shortly thereafter, there was a gentle tap on the door, and an altogether reasonable sounding voice asking if we "would come out and talk it over." As we refused the request, we noticed for the first time the cracks in the door panels, and how extremely thin the door itself seemed to be.

After a few more taps, the unwanted visitor went back to his room, from which we heard growls and grumbles. Meanwhile, we searched our room for weapons, the most intimidating of which was the small glass ash tray on the nightstand. After several more taps at our door – at about 15-minute intervals – and more requests to come out into the hall, our neighbor must've finally turned in for the night. Something we managed not to do, spending the balance of the night awaiting the next knock.

Shortly after dawn broke, we gathered our belongings and timidly ventured into the hallway, ready to make a run for it. But there was no need, as everyone else in the hotel was apparently sleeping in. Free at last of the Boston Chambers Hotel, we found a nice, and somewhat distant, spot for breakfast before resuming our sightseeing until it was time to ride the Greyhound back to Newport.

At School with the Army:
The LARC-V Amphibious Vehicle

At the completion of our mission to Newport, RI, the Tutui-la retraced its route down the stormy Atlantic seaboard to Nor-folk Naval Station and our familiar spot on Pier 2. There, in addition to the daily ship's work, we prepared for our voyage to the Far East.

Just prior to departing for what John Prine called, the "conflict overseas," I and a couple of others were temporarily assigned to the US Army. We were transported to Fort Eustis, Virginia, a few miles up the James River, to attend a training course on the engines, transmissions, and propulsion systems of a large, lumbering, and altogether curious vehicle commonly called a "Lark Five." Officially designated as LARC-V* amphibious vehicles, they were, at that time, in limited use in the northern coastal regions of South Viet Nam.

Operating principally at the far northern city of Da Nang, these vehicles – with a boat-like bottom hull, and both large balloon tires AND a propeller – could drive down a beach, en-ter the water, shift gears, and motor out to a cargo ship an-chored offshore. The LARC-V had a large central cargo well onto which materials could be loaded via the ship's crane. The vehicle would then return to the shore and drive right up the beach to its off-load point. This was proving to be quite useful at a place where there was no real harbor, lots of beach, and a quickly growing military facility.

The school was an interesting diversion, and I learned a lot about the Cummins diesel engine, and the various mechanisms which it drove, but in practical terms, I spent the entirety of my visit to Viet Nam in the central and southern parts of the coun-

---

* *Lighter, Amphibious Resupply, Cargo, 5 ton*

try, and never once laid eyes on a LARC-V amphibious vehicle – so much for forward planning.

Fort Eustis was, and is, home of the Army Transportation Corps, and with it the training facilities for the maintenance of everything from jeeps and trucks to helicopters and light aircraft. At the time I was there, virtually all of the Army personnel then in training at Fort Eustis were slated for Viet Nam. There were exceptions, however. One night at the Enlisted Men's Club we met a soldier, one of several hundred in his training unit, who was celebrating the fact that he was the only one in his unit to have instead received orders to Germany. I don't believe I have ever seen someone enjoy an evening at a military EM Club quite so much.

Our training went well and after a couple of weeks with the Army, full of newly acquired, and ultimately useless knowledge, we were returned to the Tutuila for our own journey to Viet Nam.

A Visit to Washington DC

Shortly before leaving Norfolk for the last time, as I had promised myself when passing through the capital on the eve of last Thanksgiving, I took the opportunity to pay a weekend visit to Washington DC. In those days, on the rare occasions that I would travel away from Norfolk for a day or a weekend, a Greyhound bus would take me, as it did on this weekend in early 1966. Remembering well the lessons learned during my recent night in Boston, the first thing I did upon arrival was to carefully select a safe, comfortable, yet still inexpensive, room for the night. Though the place I chose was adequate for my needs, it was perhaps the smallest, and certainly the oddest hotel room I have ever seen.

Tucked into a corner of two oddly angled hallways, in an

even more oddly shaped building, I suspected that my lodging for the night had originally been designed as a closet or small storage room. I chose to think of it as cozy, and as I have said, being both clean and secure, it appeared to be, and in fact was, perfectly satisfactory.

After checking in and dropping off my bag, I toured the city a bit to get a sense of the place before changing and taking in the local nightlife. I visited a local discotheque, and attempted to mingle with the crowd. As it turned out, strangers were not really all that welcome; at least not in that place, and not to me. The evening wasn't a total loss, however. I had a couple of drinks, chatted with a few people, and enjoyed the music and the dancing (or at least watching others do so). All of this fun notwithstanding, I decided to call it a night relatively early and returned to my room where, after sampling the local programming on the TV which was bracketed to the wall above my door, I turned in and slept quite well, thank you.

On Sunday morning, I woke, dressed in slacks, a pale yellow shirt (a color called "maize" by the salesman at the below-the-locker-club men's clothing store in Norfolk), and a nice tie. We did such things in those days when going somewhere important; and I thought a visit to the nation's capital, the White House (at least the street out front on Pennsylvania Avenue), the Lincoln Memorial, and such, were important enough to warrant a little dressing up.

After checking out, among the many other sites I visited, I headed for the Washington Monument, where I decided to forgo the elevator (and the very long line) in favor of the 897 steps to the top. About halfway up – just as I was beginning to regret my choice – I met an interesting couple of fellows. One tall, the other short, and both quite thin; they were also both *very* avant-garde. The term "hippie" might've applied, had it been in the lexicon at the time. But they were friendly, and interested in the nation's history and its monuments, and since we *were* all sharing the ordeal, we decided to walk the remaining steps together. Also, there was something about them that made me think of Simon and Garfunkel, which I thought was pretty cool.

After making it, finally, to the top, we enjoyed the spectacular view in all directions before wisely riding the elevator back to ground level. After that, I spent the next couple of hours with my new friends, walking around the city and visiting other tourist attractions, before stopping at a food stand, where I bought them each a hotdog and a Coke. I suspect that if I hadn't done so, I would've had to eat alone in front of them, but I liked them and so I was happy to treat.

We chatted and I learned a bit about a facet of modern youth culture of which I was not really aware at the time. I could tell by their dress and their attitude toward things that they occupied a world which was largely outside of my experience. In retrospect, I know this was certainly true. I had not yet visited Greenwich Village, or the North Beach District of San Francisco, or The Haight, and any experience which might be called avant-garde – other than seeing Maynard G. Krebs on TV – was not to be found in Aurora, or in Pittsburgh, or Norfolk, Virginia for that matter.

The taller one wore a small, flat, and abstract-shaped piece of polished wood on a chain around his neck. I would have thought it kind of looked like the Nike "swoosh," had I known then what that would someday be. So I asked him what it was.

"A symbol," he replied. "Of what?" I asked.

"Oh, I don't know. Just a symbol for all of the things that need symbols, but don't have one."

How can you disagree with that?

We parted company after a bit, and shortly thereafter, I met three lovely Midwestern girls my age; we shared a taxi tour which took us to Arlington National Cemetery. I enjoyed seeing and experiencing this very much, but would not have thought to visit, but for my *new*, new friends. The driver was great. He not only showed us the famous sites, but lesser known features, as well – many of which we wouldn't have even known about (i.e., the main mast from the battleship, the USS Maine) – and explained their significance. He also timed the tour, and positioned us in precisely the right spot to get the best view of the changing of the guard at the Tomb of the Unknown Soldier – very impressive.

The taxi ride back to DC deposited me at the bus station, where I bid the girls farewell and went inside to await my bus back to Norfolk.

Final Weekend in Norfolk – A Rock Show

On the last weekend before the Tutuila's final departure from Pier 2 and Norfolk, I attended a "Rock and Roll Show" at the Norfolk Municipal Auditorium. The show featured, among several others, Paul Revere and the Raiders, Gary Lewis & the Playboys, The Bobby Fuller Four, and Billy Joe Royal. All in all, it was quite a lineup, and very entertaining for several reasons.

The auditorium was an old-style theater with a broad stage whose front edge rose about three feet above the theater floor, and was set about 10 feet back from the first row of seats. The seating area then sloped sharply upward to the entrances along the back wall, and was defined by two side aisles, at the walls, and a wide center aisle.

The attendance was exceptional. The capacity crowd consisted mostly of teenage girls, each with an Instamatic camera and an adequate supply of Flashcubes. Perhaps thoughts of Elvis or Beatles performances were in the minds of the local management, because before the show began, we were warned quite sternly that everyone must stay in their seat, and that no one would be allowed to congregate in the center aisle or at the edge of the stage. This rule, we were told, would be rigidly enforced.

The show began, and as one erstwhile teen idol after another performed on stage, the girls were getting restless. Finally one brave girl, camera in hand, charged down the center aisle, screeched to a halt at the edge of the stage and snapped a picture. She immediately turned and bolted up the aisle and back to her seat. There was nothing at that point for security to do; the deed was done, order was restored, and all was again well.

But the precedent had been set. Shortly after, another girl charged the stage, snapped a picture and quickly returned to her seat. And then another. And then another. After a while, pictures weren't enough. The girls – now sometimes passing each other on their way to and from the stage – were writing notes of endearment, which they balled up and tossed to the foot of whoever was their favorite.

By this time, the headliners, Paul Revere and the Raiders, were performing, and as notes would roll up to their feet, Paul Revere or lead singer Mark Lindsay would, between songs, pick up one or two and read them aloud; each causing a squeal of delight from someone in the otherwise anonymous crowd.

Encouraged, one brave girl took it a step further. Like others before her, she charged the stage, but didn't stop. A few feet short of the stage, she launched herself and performed an admirable belly flop, sliding and stopping at the feet of Paul Revere himself. This time the line had clearly been crossed, bringing quick action from the security people in the stage wings. But before they could arrive at mid-stage, the girl had leapt to her feet and wrapped her arms tightly around Paul Revere. Now, as the security people arrived to drag her away, the most wonderful thing happened. Paul also wrapped *his* arms around *her* and would not let go, thus thwarting the best efforts of the brutes.

This went on for a couple of minutes before Paul Revere,

seemingly reluctantly, allowed the security people to escort her to the side of the stage. To those of us in the audience, she was a hero, and I'm hoping, and suspecting, that whatever consequences she paid for her actions were minimal compared with her experience. Whatever the cost, I'm sure it was worth it.

Later in the show we got a contrary lesson on the arrogance of some performers. Gary Lewis, son of the more famous Jerry Lewis, was performing when again a girl charged the stage and threw a note so well aimed that it touched his shoe before stopping. Rather than acknowledging, or reading the note, or simply just ignoring it, he glanced down and, with his toe, kicked the note away. I don't know, but I can imagine how this girl must've felt. As for me, I never again liked, or listened to, his music. Hearing it will forever remind me of that moment.

But all in all, the show was great fun, and a nice final experience in a city which, in truth, I didn't really like all that much. However, my feelings toward Norfolk no longer mattered, as early the following Tuesday morning we cast off from Pier 2 for the last time, the beginning of a four-leg journey which would take us to the other side of the world.

To Viet Nam – and Home Again

En Route to Viet Nam – The Panama Canal

The USS Tutuila departed Norfolk, Virginia for the last time and steamed the now familiar route to the Caribbean, and when we got there we sailed right on through. We crossed the Caribbean Sea – north to south – and arrived at Limon Bay, the "eastern" terminus of the Panama Canal. We were scheduled to spend two days waiting for our reserved time to transverse the waterway to the Pacific Ocean. This meant liberty in the Panamanian city of Colón, which we later discovered was not a place we really wanted to visit. And fortunately we did not.

Shortly after we arrived and dropped anchor amidst the many commercial freighters awaiting their turn, a slot opened up for us. So that afternoon we weighed anchor and began our journey through the canal to the Pacific end which, owing to the orientation of the continent joining Isthmus, and the angle of the canal itself, lay some 50 miles to the south and east of where we now were. Getting underway, we entered a narrow passage which took us to the Gatun Locks, where the ship was raised about 85 feet to the level of the inland waterway.

Moving through the Panama Canal's famous locks was a tedious and time-consuming, but also very interesting, process. Repair Division personnel had no part to play in the actual movement of the ship so we were all free to watch as the ship carefully positioned itself into the lock and tied up. When the water level was properly adjusted, and the great doors opened, docking lines were untied and we were pulled forward by two very large locomotives and debauched into Gatun Lake. Crossing this jungle bound lake would take us about halfway across the isthmus.

As we waited for the water – and with it, of course, the ship – to rise (or to lower on the Pacific side) Panamanians, mostly children and adolescents, would come up to the walls of the lock, just a couple of feet from the port side of the ship. They came to sell trinkets and souvenirs to the otherwise idle sailors. I bought, for 50 cents I think, a brightly colored satin doily, with embroidered canal scenes and fringe on the edges, which I sent home to my mother.

As we left the locks behind and steamed into Gatun Lake, it was almost dark, and when Lights-Out and Taps were later sounded, they marked an end to our last day on the eastern side of the continent. When Reveille was sounded the next morning, we were up and off to the mess decks for breakfast. It was then that I got my first look at a "steaming jungle." As the sun rose above the mountainous rain forests surrounding the lake, steam quite literally rose from within the bright green canopy.

As the lower part of the lake narrowed to become the Rio Chagres, we came increasingly closer to the primeval shoreline. As we stared in wonder, I recalled being told of the quantity and variety of animal life within that dense jungle, most of which we didn't actually see, but which we knew were there and not very far away. Among these were about a billion insects, crocodiles, and other reptiles, including a frightening panoply of serpents. Also monkeys large and small, as well as a variety of large cats and other mammals, many of whom the cats routine-ly ate. This was all a bit disconcerting, but fascinating when dis-cussed from the safety of the ship.

After a long crossing of Gatun Lake and passage down the Rio Chagres, we bent south at the town of Gamboa and entered a series of cuts (the small canals famously carved through the jungle in the 1900s), which took us to the Miraflores Lake and Locks, and eventually under the Bridge of the Americas – the Pan-American Highway. Soon after, we tied up at the Port of Balboa, the docks of Panama City, for our delayed two days of liberty.

Panama City and the Pacific Ocean

After passage through the Panama Canal, we stopped for two full days in Panama City, Panama. The city was tropical, like the islands of the Caribbean, but also large and crowded, and very urban, with both affluent areas and teeming slums. The enter-tainment we would seek while ashore on our brief visit was focused squarely between the two.

One memory, which has stayed with me quite clearly, is of a downtown intersection patrolled by police in starched green uniforms, carrying submachine guns. That alone informed us that our status as US Navy personnel notwithstanding, we were in fact visiting a police state, and that we would be wise to behave accordingly.

We visited bars, of course, and roamed the streets, sightseeing and experiencing the exotic locale. All in all, if it wasn't a good time, it was an interesting one. But after the brief and dubious entertainments of Panama City, we were soon back aboard, de-parting for places further to the west.

Leaving the Port of Balboa, where the Tutuila had docked, we steamed through the Gulf of Panama and on into what author Herman Wouk once described as the humid blue void of the Pacific Ocean. This next leg of our journey would take us to Pearl Harbor, Hawaii. The voyage from Panama to Hawaii – and later the somewhat longer leg from Hawaii to Subic Bay in the Philippines – was a bit tedious. The Tutuila's top speed, if she strained a bit, was 11 knots (roughly 10 mph), a speed we didn't come close to as we crossed the vast ocean.

Additionally, we sometimes slowed or paused for drills, including man overboard drills, during which the ship stopped dead in the water as the complete event was simulated. The entire ship's company would be called to muster and counted, while the small boat crew launched and practiced a rescue several hundred yards astern.

When we eventually reached our next destination, we were almost surprised to, at last, see land.

Pearl Harbor, Hawaii

Despite the long days crossing the empty, gently heaving Pacific Ocean, we did eventually steam past Diamond Head and Waikiki, and entered the channel leading to the naval base at Pearl Harbor. As we rounded Holokahiki Point, and the western end of Hickam Air Force Base, which had been fixed in my childhood memory by the old World War II movies as Hickam Field, we steamed into Pearl Harbor itself and tied up to a pier in the Southeast Loch.

This was all very exciting; for I knew my history. In addition to the events of the "Day of Infamy," the entire Pacific war had thereafter been staged and commanded from this place and so it was, for me, quite a thrill to actually be there.

Aside from liberty in Honolulu and beyond, one thing we made sure to do was take the tourist launch to the USS Arizona Memorial, the sobering, and hauntingly beautiful monument that straddles the sunken battleship, whose main deck lies just inches below the surface of the harbor's crystal waters. There we gazed in awe at the once mighty vessel – in its day, the iconic symbol of US naval power – and we read, in solemn silence, the names etched into the monument's far wall. Names of the sailors entombed in the sunken hull below.

History and the ghosts of past events are still strong in this place.

A Tour of Oahu

While I was attending Engineman School at Great Lakes Naval Training Center, the fellow who slept above me in the double bunks of our barracks was named Roger; a nice, handsome young man, with a laid-back tropic-island personality. Roger was, in fact, from Hawaii, a resident of the city of Kaneohe on Oahu's Northeast coast.

While not particularly close friends, we got along well enough, and by the time we graduated and went our separate ways, Roger had told me and some others that if our service ever took us to Pearl Harbor, we should contact his mother and she would show us the sites.

So when the Tutuila finally lumbered into Pearl Harbor, and liberty commenced, I called Roger's mother. I wasn't quite sure what to expect, but it certainly wasn't the delight I heard in her voice to be talking to a friend of her far distant son. If we would come to Kaneohe, she quickly told me, on our next free day, she would take us around the island and indeed show us the sites.

So on the decided upon day, my shipboard friends, Robert and Jake, and I boarded a bus to take us over the Pali to Kaneohe, where Roger's mother, a wonderful lady named Diane, awaited our arrival.

She had set aside the entire day to give us a very thorough

tour of the island of Oahu, not as tourists, but from an is-
lander's perspective. From Kaneohe, we traced Oahu's north
shore, viewing places whose names were known to me through
the pop music of my high school years; Sunset Beach, Waimea,
and the spot of the Banzai Pipeline.

We turned inland and drove through miles of pineapple fields
(where it was understandably forbidden to stop and take a sam-
ple). From a distance, we saw Schofield Barracks, also known to
me from history, and from the book, *From Here to Eternity*.

Driving to the south shore and Honolulu, we visited the
National Cemetery, within the crater of an extinct volcano
(Punch Bowl). There we stopped at the simple grave of the
famous World War II correspondent, Ernie Pyle. Further east,
we rounded Diamond Head, and stopped to see the "Blow
Hole" near the extinct crater of Koko Head.

We visited a relatively small beach at an eastern shore spot
known as Hanauma Bay, formed by an extinct crater whose
eastern half has been eroded away by the sea. This place seemed
to us to be paradise itself. Mostly unknown to tourists, at the
time, it was a favorite of local islanders, and the backdrop for
parts of Elvis's movie, *Blue Hawaii*.

An unhurried drive up the eastern shoreline then took us
back to Kaneohe, and the end of one of the best days I have
ever had. Thanks Diane and Roger.

Honolulu and Waikiki

On liberty from the Tutuila, my friends and I mostly passed
on the questionable pleasures of Honolulu's traditional Navy
haunts – Chinatown and the infamous Hotel Street. Rather, we
spent most of our time in the Hawaii most known at the time
to tourists – Waikiki Beach and its surroundings.

A portion of land between Kalakaua Avenue and the ocean –

within the parameters of Waikiki Beach – was owned by the US Army. And so the Fort DeRussy portion of Waikiki was limited to military personnel and guests. This was good for everyone, as beach and recreational facilities at Fort DeRussy were more than adequate and well located on the famous expanse of beach, with Diamond Head looming in the background.

We were welcome there and could settle in to a prime spot without having to impose on the minimal hospitality of the big hotels. And the hotels, in turn, didn't have to put up with us tromping through and trying to take up space intended for paying guests. At the water's edge, however, the sandy strip of beach itself was public land, so we weren't restricted from walking the beach to the hotels, where girls might be.

Not surprisingly, we had a pretty good time. When not on the beach we walked Waikiki's main street, Kalakaua Avenue, which runs parallel to the ocean. On one side were the famous beachfront hotels, and on the other were many tourist attractions. We visited the International Marketplace; really just a mall – but an exotic one, and in a prime location. We even entered the famous nightclub Duke Kahanamoku's, and actually saw Don Ho (Tiny Bubbles) on stage before we were turned around, shown the door, and encouraged to use it.

We weren't misbehaving; we were just a small group of enlisted sailors in uniform. And in Waikiki's upper social strata and tourist environment, we were considered somewhat déclassé. So we moved on. That was okay; there was plenty of fun to be had, and we didn't really want to spend our time sitting in a fancy nightclub anyway.

A Most Famous Person

During the time the Tutuila was visiting Pearl Harbor, a major local holiday occurred. I had not previously known of

Kamehameha Day, which honors Kamehameha I, the former unifier (in 1810) and King of the Hawaiian Islands; a revered figure in Hawaiian culture, past and present.

All of Honolulu, it seemed, had shut down for Kamehameha Day, and huge crowds gathered along King Street and beyond for the annual parade. There were floats from all parts of the island group, all made of local flowers, sort of like a Polynesian Rose Bowl parade. Along with the floats were open cars with local celebrities riding high and waving, marchers from local societies, high school marching bands, and others (in other words, all of the elements of a major holiday parade anywhere). The parade elements mustered and marched, seemingly endlessly, from the starting point, past the Iolani Palace (the former royal residence of Hawaii's historical rulers), and off into the distance. It was directly in front of the palace that our guide, Diane, had recommended as the best place to view the festivities, and so here, at the edge of the roadway, we stood.

We soon discovered that behind us in the palace, on the governor's balcony, along with the governor and other VIPs, was a national celebrity. Visiting (and actually living on the island for a brief time) was Jacqueline Kennedy, and her children, nine-year-old Caroline and six-year-old "John John."

I will admit it was a thrill to actually see them in person, viewing the events from their vantage point, two stories up and perhaps 50 yards behind where we stood in the crush at curbside.

The parade, eventually, came to an end, and as Robert, Jake, and I were starting to move on, a ripple of excitement passed through the crowd. The rumor was that Mrs. Kennedy and the children would be leaving the palace grounds in a limo, passing through a gate located on the cross street just ahead of us. We didn't know if this was true, but we were going in that direction anyway, so we joined the gathering throng outside the gate.

By the time we actually got there we were well back from the gate, and tall as I am not, I couldn't see over most of those in front of me. But I got an idea. Disregarding how far back I was, I positioned myself in the center of the drive and waited. When the time came, the first persons out of the gate were, of course, swarms of security, pushing people off of the drive itself and out of the limo's intended path. As the crowds parted, or were pushed back, I held my ground as others backed up. Finally, when directly confronted by an officer, I backed up until he was satisfied with my position – at the edge of the drive, front row.

As the limo slowly moved past, I was close enough (although I did not) to touch the car as I bent and peered through the window at who, at the time, was perhaps the most famous woman and certainly the most sympathized and revered person in the country.

In that moment, my previous thrill at actually seeing them was repeated and multiplied as I gaped and gawked like everyone else, secretly proud of the maneuver which had provided me with such an extraordinary view. My two friends, who had moved at the first instruction to do so, barely got a look at the car.

Crossing the Pacific – Subic Bay, The Philippines

On the long voyage to the Western Pacific we steamed through waters, and past islands (usually unseen), which had been fiercely contested not so many years before. As we progressed, I had a strong sense of the old war movies and books, telling of the struggles and triumphs in the Central Pacific and in the Philippine Sea through which we passed.

In due time, we rounded the bight of Luzon's northwest coast, and steamed down the island's western side to Subic Bay, where we had the opportunity to rest, recreate, and finally touch actual land once again. The large natural harbor of Subic Bay was a significant naval base which had been acquired by the

US after the Spanish-American War, and retained by treaty after Philippine independence. It had also been used to their advantage by the Japanese Navy from early 1942, until they were rudely dislodged by US forces at the end of 1944.

Our stop at Subic Bay and the nearby community was an eye-opener. Although I had spent time ashore in San Juan and other parts of Puerto Rico, and just recently in Panama City Panama, nothing could have prepared me for our descent into the series of third world environments which we were now beginning. Parts of Panama City should've been a clue, but for the most part, it was a large, urban, and somewhat modern environment. If we had docked in Manila, I'm certain our experience would've been comparable.

But the only liberty available beyond the confines of the naval base at Subic Bay was the town of Olongapo, and then only the main streets of Magsaysay Drive and Rizal Avenue were "on limits." This was the Philippine version of the "Strip," examples of which exist just outside any military facility, and which catered to the off-base "needs" of its personnel. The remainder of the town was considered by military authorities to be troublesome for visiting sailors and marines – if not downright dangerous.

The first taste (and smell) of this reality came immediately after passing through the naval station's main gate.

Olongapo City

The small waterway separating the Subic Bay Naval Station from the adjacent community was a natural stream, ultimately debauching into the bay itself. At some point however, the stream had been co-opted for a greater purpose, and became known officially as a "drainage canal." It was commonly, and correctly, referred to as "S**t River" by those who crossed the bridge connecting the main gate to the town.

Most, if not all, of the town sewage – open or only occasionally otherwise, it seemed – made its way into the canal and under the bridge on its journey to the bay. It was truly a strange sensation to be holding your nose and trying not to breathe, while at the same time seeing the local children swimming in the murky water – and occasionally diving for coins tossed by what *I thought* to be callous sailors and marines standing above.

Once over the bridge, where we could breathe again, we immediately encountered the reality of Magsaysay Avenue which consisted of a seemingly endless row of bars and bar girls – which requires no further explanation. There were also souvenir shops, and various street vendors whose offerings included watches, cameras, knives, and "monkey meat on a stick."

This last was actually a popular snack, usually enjoyed while strolling from one amusement to the next. Enterprising locals would go into the nearby jungle, and return with a monkey, whose cubed meat they would skewer and cook – right on the sidewalk – over a couple of charcoal briquettes in a two-pound coffee can. It was inexpensive, and actually pretty tasty when thoroughly cooked, which more than occasionally it was not. The only downside to enjoying our snack as we strolled along was that some of the feeder streams to the drainage canal ran through board covered breaks in the sidewalk, so we occasionally had to stop eating and hold our noses as we quickly moved along.

As enjoyable as all of this was, there *was* entertainment available on the base, as well. One day, two friends and I discovered that a small fishing boat could be rented, along with the appropriate bait and tackle, from a facility on the bay's shore near the Enlisted Men's Club. This we did, and soon we were motoring past the Tutuila and other anchored ships into the vast solitude of the mountain-fringed, and actually quite beautiful, bay.

There, included in the panorama, we could watch planes taking off in the distance from Clark Air Force Base, bound for missions over Viet Nam. But mostly we spent the afternoon drifting about and fishing in a somewhat desultory way, enjoying the uniqueness and isolation of the situation – and perhaps consuming reasonable quantities of some beverage.

After our brief pause at Subic Bay, we weighed anchor and departed. Our voyage this time would be short, as we steamed across the South China Sea on a diagonal northeast to southwest, and rounded the southern tip of Viet Nam. Once in the Gulf of Thailand, we steamed north to our destination, the village – and patrol boat base – at An Thoi.

Viet Nam: An Thoi, Part One

Not too much to say about Viet Nam actually. First, three months at An Thoi, home of PCF (Swift Boat) Division 101 and Coast Guard Division 11, located at the southern tip of Phu Quoc Island. The village of An Thoi was actually in Cambodian coastal water, but for some reason, the offshore border curved to the west, making all of Phu Quoc part of the Republic of Viet Nam. The patrol boat base at An Thoi was originally a US Coast Guard facility, with some South Vietnamese craft and a

Thai gunboat for good measure. These were joined – almost a year prior to Tutuila's arrival – by the boats of PCF 101.

The facility at An Thoi was officially designated as a "Coastal Surveillance Force Combat and Logistical Base" where, in addition to our shipboard duties, we occasionally supplemented the five-man Swift Boat crews. An Thoi's boats – the 50-foot PCFs and the 82-foot Coast Guard Cutters, were responsible for stopping (or slowing) the water-born supply of men and materials to the Viet Cong from nearby Cambodia. Also for patrol and interdiction along Viet Nam's Gulf (of Thailand) coast, from the Cambodian border, south past the city of Rach Gia and the U-Minh Forest, to Ca Mau Cape, the southernmost point of the country. In addition to the boat base, the area around An Thoi included a sizable community of civilian construction workers, a small airstrip, and a nearby prisoner of war camp. The island also included a surprising number of Viet Cong, given its separation from the mainland of Viet Nam.

Arriving at An Thoi to relieve the USS Krishna, the Tutuila anchored just offshore, rafting with an APL – Auxiliary-Personnel-Living, in Navy parlance – which served as both headquarters and barracks for the Swift Boat crews. There the "Toot" served as principal repair facility, not just for PCF 101, and Coast Guard Division 11, but potentially for all US naval craft on the gulf side of South Viet Nam.

Shortly after our arrival, some of us were briefly pressed into service as crew – coxswains, boat engineers, and bow hooks – as Tutuila participated in Operation Sea-Mount, an effort to clear enemy forces from the southern parts of the island, using our LCM (Landing Craft, Mechanized) landing craft to transport Army troops in four WWII-style beach assaults at various places on the Phu Quoc coast.

Of the activity at An Thoi itself, one of the things I remember most is an event which did not happen. A touring USO troupe, featuring Sue Thompson, a popular singer at the time with several hits including "Norman," "Paper Tiger," and the weepy "Sad Movies Always Make Me Cry," was scheduled to perform for us (and the civilians) at the facility in An Thoi.

We were all very much looking forward to the diversion, the presence of the adorable Sue Thompson, and whatever additional girls might be part of the show. Alas, it was not to be, for around 3 am on the morning of their scheduled arrival, the airstrip took three Viet Cong mortar rounds, which caused no real damage other than to get the USO show canceled.

As to the war itself, there was an expression in the Army at the time, which may or may not have been true: "Nine out of ten times, it's a walk in the woods." Activities at An Thoi were something like that in the earlier days; though boats on patrol had occasional scary moments and the ship and the APL were always tempting targets for sappers, which required constant vigil.

Viet Nam: An Thoi, Part Two

Notwithstanding the grueling work schedule, there were occasional lulls, and despite the near-total isolation of An Thoi, we did find a few diversions and some entertainment, in addition to the almost nightly movie aboard the APL – which we occasionally had time to attend.

Just south of An Thoi was a chain of several small islands. One of these, about a half-mile long, with two peaks and a low saddle in the middle provided two popular diversions. On the eastern side, at the low point, was a small but fantastic beach. It was to this perfect half-circle of white sand, bracketed by lush green jungle and crystal clear water that we would come, when circumstances allowed – and we could acquire a boat for a swimming party.

On the western side of the island, opposite the beach, was a tiny fishing village, so remote and insignificant, that it remained untouched by the war. A few hundred yards through the jungle, a somewhat overgrown path would take us to not only a different culture, but a different time. With the exception of a small boat with an ancient motor, in which the village leaders transported their cargos of dried fish to An Thoi, the village pretty much existed in an 18th-century environment. Here, we would entertain ourselves by watching the villagers work, and bartering for such novelties as the long, toothy, snouts removed from the sawfish that the villagers caught, and for strips of fish, sun-dried on bamboo frames, which were the principal product of the village.

By chance, I recently discovered on YouTube that same beach, which is now the focal point of a major resort, a popular vacation destination for people as far away as Australia. Although I almost certainly will not, I would like to visit that tiny island again and see how it is changed – but, in truth, I would really rather again see the pristine paradise that it was then.

Bangkok Thailand – R & R

After three months of hard work, and no small number of sleepless nights repairing, rebuilding, or installing engines to keep An Thoi's Swift Boats online, the Tutuila was relieved and assigned to similar duty near Cat Lo, at the mouth of the Saigon River.

But first a short visit to Bangkok, Thailand. We were already in the Gulf of Thailand, so Bangkok was a logical choice for a bit of R & R. The Tutuila weighed anchor and set a northeast course for the Bay of Bangkok. At the appropriate longitude, she turned and steamed north through the bay. Without pause, we continued up the Chao Phraya River to the city, about 18 miles from the coast. Our actual inland travel distance was about twice that, however, as we followed the many twists and turns of the river, which at that point was the main channel of a wide delta.

Finally, with Bangkok all around us, we anchored midstream in the swiftly flowing river, which was crowded with both small boats and chunks of vegetation – from various branches to portions of whole trees – which had been dislodged somehow from the dense jungle upstream and were now making their rapid journey to the sea.

This ancient Siamese capital of perhaps five million people was divided nearly in half by the broad and raging river, but incredibly, there were no bridges connecting the exotic, but relatively modern city on the east bank to the more densely populated, more traditional – and swampier – western sectors.

Consequently, along with the vegetation the river teemed with boat traffic of all kinds. Whether they were water taxis transporting passengers, or the waterborne equivalent of trucks carrying goods across the river and through the numerous canals, boats were everywhere. Prominent among the watercraft were a type of boat I've seen nowhere else in the world. Long and narrow, these boats were the hotrods of Bangkok's waterways. Used I'm sure for recreation, these speedboats were also employed as an inexpensive alternative for transporting passengers – tourist and locals – from one side of the river to the other.

The most curious feature of these vessels was the propulsion system. Just behind the raised driver's platform at the aft end of the boat was a V-8 automobile engine, mounted on a swivel post with a long propeller shaft behind and a control/steering bar projecting forward. The driver would rev the engine and tilt the engine up, thus dipping the propeller into the water and off they would go, leaping forward into the waves. Controlling the propeller's depth allowed the boats to sometimes access very shallow water in the areas around the city.

It was quickly determined that this was how we were going

to get about. Almost anywhere on either side of the river, it was
easy to find such a boat waiting for passengers at the bank. For
50 cents, up to six of us would climb aboard and be taken on a
rather exciting journey to wherever we chose to go. Not only
cheap and convenient, but great fun!

Bangkok Thailand – Tourists in Uniform

Aside from seeking out the nightlife for which Bangkok was,
and is, rightly famous, we also, as you might expect, did a lot of
touristy things as well.

We visited Wat Arun, or "Temple of Dawn," a spectacular
edifice on the west bank of the river, opposite downtown. The
282-foot porcelain-encrusted central tower dominates the landscape, and actually glows in the early morning sunlight.

The square, ornate, and gradually narrowing central tower is
accessible to climbers almost all the way to the top via narrow
stone steps built into the outer surfaces of each side. Getting up
wasn't too difficult, but upon reaching the summit, I had to face
the reality of getting back down. At that moment, I was standing in the open air, high above the safety of the ground, on a
stone step which was not quite as deep as the length of my feet,
with a couple of hundred such steps to go. I'm not quite sure
why I went up to begin with – beyond the fact that all of my
friends did – as I'm not all that comfortable with unsecured
heights. Obviously, I did eventually make it back down, but it
was a harrowing effort.

We decided to forego the speedboats for once and took a
tourist launch to, among other places, one of the floating mar-
kets for which the city was, even then, quite famous. These exist
in the klongs (canals) on the western side of the river. Entering
the west bank waterways, we passed through the residential
neighborhoods lining the canals until suddenly, we were in the

midst of a "business district." With restaurants and shops on the banks, the canal itself was jammed with what seemed to be a hundred small boats, many riding low in the water, laden with goods for sale. Others, sometimes just large enough for a single person, carried customers. The merchandise available, sold from boat to boat, was mostly agricultural products grown locally, and tropical flowers of every imaginable type and color.

On another day, on the eastern side of the river, we visited the Temple of the Golden Buddha, a not so large, but grand and ornate structure housing an enormous statue of the Buddha, made of approximately five tons of brightly polished solid gold. The Buddha was "discovered" by westerners during the colonial period, and was at the time encased – for safekeeping – in a gold painted layer of concrete. One day, a piece of the concrete was broken away, exposing the secret hidden within. Science confirmed that it was, in fact, solid gold, through and through.

We stood in awe of the beauty, and the majesty of the glittering gold icon, but what seemed most amazing to me was the openness of it all. It may be different today, but at the time, anyone could simply walk in and step up to the low fence which was almost within reach of the statue itself. There, one could leave an offering, pray, or simply stand and (respectfully) gawk at the altogether remarkable visage.

Bangkok Thailand – The Royal Palace

But most remarkable of all was a visit to the royal palace, and within the palace grounds, the Temple of the Emerald Buddha. This was itself a large structure, but contained no community of monks. This was, in fact, the personal temple of the royal family, and contained, high on a secure platform, within an even more secure glass case, the 30-inch high Emerald Buddha.

Named for its color, the "image" of the Buddha was actually

crafted in 43 BC from a single, flawless piece of Green Jasper. Discounting both the artistic and religious significance of the Golden Buddha, its worldly value (as gold) could be easily calculated. The value of the Emerald Buddha, on the other hand, is said to be beyond measure.

I would have liked to taken my Instamatic camera onto the palace grounds, and into the temple. I wish I had pictures of the Buddha, and the many, many other really beautiful things both inside and outside of the temple. Alas, this was not permitted – particularly for Americans. The ban was explained to us as follows. The King of Thailand, a young man at the time who, given Siamese history, rightly took his position seriously. Although Thailand is a great friend of the United States, the king had recently viewed Yul Brenner playing the King of Siam in a Hollywood movie. The real king was greatly offended by two things shown in that movie. One, Yul Brenner, as the King of Siam, sat on a cushion on the floor, thus allowing others' heads to be higher than his own. This was not allowed in real life. And two, when the movie king ate, he ate with chopsticks. It was pointed out to us that the Siamese of that period were a civilized people who had used spoons. It was those primitive Chinese who did, and still do, use chopsticks.

"Snake Farm"

I have, as I earlier reported, a severe phobia of snakes. It seems strange, but for a brief period, I was able to put my phobia aside. While I was in Viet Nam, encounters with snakes were all too possible. At the same time, you definitely did not want your comrades knowing you had a phobia of any kind. So, while I was there I simply didn't have a phobia – to the extent that I actually visited a "snake farm" while in Bangkok.

This facility was run by the International Red Cross, and was the principal source of anti-venom serum for most of Southeast Asia. It was, and still is, a major tourist attraction. There you could gaze into several large, walled concrete pits, perhaps 50 feet in diameter, complete with water and some low vegetation to simulate a habitat. Each pit was halved by a wall, and each half was full, I mean FULL, of some kind of serpent indigenous to that part of the world – mostly cobras, kraits, and other types of vipers.

There was a demonstration of "milking" a cobra to extract venom, and a show in which a small Thai man stood eye to eye with an enraged king cobra in a "bullfighting-like" activity, which was entertaining and quite exciting. I thoroughly enjoyed it all.

Alas, when I returned home, the phobia came back with me.*

Viet Nam – Vung Tau

After three months at An Thoi, and five days of R & R in Bangkok, the ship moved to support PCF Division 103, and Coast Guard Division 13 located at Cat Lo. This brought us into the environs of Vung Tao, a former French resort city at the mouth of the Saigon River and the northern boundary of the Mekong Delta.

Perched on a headland, Vung Tau's "back side" was the southern end of about 300 miles of what are among the most beautiful beaches in that part of the world. This is certainly one of the reasons why the French colonial masters chose Vung Tau – which they then called Cap Saint-Jacques – for a resort, and

---

* *About ten years ago my brother visited Milwaukee and we spent an afternoon at the Milwaukee Zoo. He wanted to see the Reptile House – which he did, while I waited at what I hoped to be a safe distance of about 50 yards.*

perhaps why MACV* chose the place as the location of the Army's In-Country R & R facility.

It was here that we supported the Swift Boat and Coast Guard Divisions at Cat Lo, and sometimes the B-Class Mine-sweepers stationed at Nhà Bè, who were always busy keeping the river clear for ship traffic from Saigon to the coast. We were also available to service any other vessels that came along requiring expert attention.

A principal focus of small boat activity, and that of the soon to arrive Ninth Infantry Division, centered on the nearby Rung Sat Swamp (or Special Zone), from which the Viet Cong would occasionally swarm, and which was an ideal place to hide and attack ship traffic on the River.

When the 2nd Brigade of the 9th Infantry was assigned to the Mobile Riverine Force, the Tutuila assumed a support role for those boats in the Vung Tau area, and aided in the preparation of the ASPB, or "Alpha" Boats, and other craft.

When the time came, it was from Vung Tau that I began my journey home.

Returning to the World: Part One – Waiting to Leave

Early in 1967, along with 164 others, I flew on a World Airlines 707 from the air base at Bien Hoa, Republic of Viet Nam to Travis Air Force Base in northern California. Leaving the plane at Travis, confronted by seemingly endless rows of B-52 bombers and the Sierra Nevada Mountains in the distance, I began my return to "The World."

The flight, indeed the entire preceding week, had been something of a twilight zone experience. After being detached, I flew

---

* *Military Assistance Command – Viet Nam*

from the airstrip at nearby Vung Tau on a twin-engine Army transport to Ton Son Nhut Air Base at Saigon. Bused into town, I was given lodging at the Annapolis Motel; a two-story dorm for Navy personnel nestled at the edge of a swamp on the outskirts of the city. There, I was given the appropriate number of meal vouchers and stern instructions to be on the transport to Bien Hoa, some 16 miles away, at 6 am – six days hence! Within the boundaries of curfew, and subject to a few tedious military rules, I was free to go wherever and do whatever I pleased until then.

After a day of exploring the city a bit, I was tempted to try and hitch a flight back to Vung Tau for a couple of days. I knew the town and I had a "sort-of" girlfriend there, who was at that moment, of course, busily forgetting me in favor of the next "Joe" who would buy her plenty of Saigon Tea.

> *"You buy me, Saigon Tea*
> *You no buy, you dede"*
>
> *Anonymous*

But common sense prevailed and I made do in Saigon, spending most of my days hanging out at the Ypsilanti Snack Bar, the canteen at a much larger Army housing facility, in what seemed to be a much better neighborhood. Evenings were spent in a couple of acceptable drinking establishments. The only downside was, of course, the waiting to actually go home, and the flinching in response to the many firecrackers of the Tet celebration, this being exactly one year before Tet of 1968, of which we all came to know so well.

My musical memories of my brief stay in Saigon are "Last Train to Clarksville" by the Monkees, and "If I Were a Carpen-

---

* *Dede (dee-dee) = Vietnamese for "Go Away"*

ter," by Bobby Darin. Heard from the jukebox at the Ypsilanti Snack Bar, these were the first contemporary songs I had heard in a very long time.

Returning to the World: Part Two – The Flight Home

When the great day finally arrived, there I was, with all my stuff, waiting for the ride to Bien Hoa. Because we were flying to northern California and it was still winter, I was required to wear a dress winter uniform made of heavy, dark blue wool. Very comfortable in the winter, except that the temperature in Bien Hoa that day topped out at 95° Fahrenheit. Fortunately, it was a dry heat.

We arrived at the air base at about 8 am. The plane departed promptly at 5:45 pm. Was it the longest day of my life? Yes, it was, but a busy one. We were processed, searched, examined, lectured to, fed, lectured to again, processed some more, and finally herded to an open area to wait. This last was easy, because we had waited, usually in the sun, before every event of the day and we were well-practiced.

The search turned out to be the most interesting part of the day. It was mainly to keep us from taking prohibited items home with us. This was a major feature of the lectures as well, and focused primarily on three things: liquor above the allowed amount, dope, and weapons and/or ammunition. These latter in any amounts at all. What was really surprising and often amusing was the amount of all of the above that was found and confiscated that day. Lots, and lots, and lots of booze, of course, not so much dope, this being early in the war, but plenty of the other stuff – an AK-47, grenades, plenty of live rounds in many calibers, and amazingly, two live Claymore mines!

After a long, hot day in the sun, in our winter uniforms, we boarded the plane for home and departed Bien Hoa without incident. Whew! As the wheels left the ground, a cheer erupted from all 165 of us – no surprise. The stewardesses were friendly and, not surprisingly, gorgeous and altogether wonderful, each and every one of them.

The first surprise of the flight came about 30 minutes after lift-off when a soldier asked for a drink of water. After a few moments, we were informed that there was no drinking water aboard – no water, no coffee, no tea, or soda, or nearly anything else. The consolation was, to our great relief, there was plenty of pineapple juice. After hearing that there was no water on the plane, we were all immediately very thirsty, but of course we had plenty of sweet, sticky pineapple juice. I must say, the stewardesses were great. They absorbed plenty of mostly good-natured abuse for the remaining four hours to Tokyo, where we were properly re-supplied.

The next surprise was that at the Tokyo airport it was SNOWING!! And the temperature was a shocking cold 28° Fahrenheit. A couple of chilly hours at the Tokyo airport and we were off and eastward bound. No cheers this time, but with thirsts quenched, we settled in for the long leg of the flight, spent mostly asleep.

About 18 hours later, we discovered that we were over land. Someone speculated, probably correctly, that it was Oregon below us and that it would not be long now. And so it was that an hour or so later we landed at Travis AFB. All I had to do at this point was to sweat out the mustering out process and go home – as a civilian!

Homecoming – Delayed in San Francisco

Returning at last from Viet Nam, I don't know what became of the Army fellows after we deplaned at Travis Air Force Base, but the one other sailor and I were directed to a Navy bus and driven to Treasure Island, a naval facility on an island in San Francisco Bay. It seems a bit strange to say, but I hadn't really been keeping track of what day it was, and when I checked in at T.I., I discovered it was late Friday afternoon. I was assigned a bunk and told the mustering out process would begin promptly Monday morning. History repeated itself, and once again, I checked into a naval facility only to be told that I was not needed, or even required to be there, for several days.

After finding my bunk and stowing my gear, I immediately caught a city bus to downtown San Francisco. I got off the bus on Market Street and simply wandered around for the next couple of hours, amazed at the thought of actually being in an American city. I stopped at a small hotdog place to get something to eat, and in doing so, discovered what was to become my home base for the next week or so. I met some people there who quickly became friends. Hanging out with them, sitting in a booth, talking, flirting with the girls, and listening to music on the jukebox was just the kind of thing that people of my age did in real life, and that I had missed for so long.

Add to this the fact that I was in San Francisco in early 1967, one of the most beautiful and interesting cities in the world – at one of the most interesting times in that city's history. At the hotdog place, I remember the music on the jukebox – "I'm A Believer" by The Monkees, "Poor Side of Town" by Johnny Rivers, but the song that would captivate me long after I went home was Scott McKenzie singing "San Francisco (Be Sure to Wear Some Flowers in Your Hair)," for this was 1967 and the beginning of the Summer of Love, well before it all turned bad.

Monday morning came, and over the next couple of days, the mustering out process ran its course. I was shuffled around a bit, given some money,* and released into the world. Even though I was free, I stayed in San Francisco for several more days before the desire to go home overwhelmed me.

I know my mother believed that I returned home as quickly as I could, and it would have broken her heart had she known that I had delayed my return. But I had fallen in love with San Francisco, and as wonderful as it was to go home to my family and friends, it was hard to leave. Later that year, I would hear Glenn Yarbrough sing Rod McKuen's "So Long, San Francisco," and the pull would be irresistible.

Homecoming Realized – A Spaghetti Dinner

I landed at O'Hare Airport at about 8 pm on a Saturday evening. In those pre-security days, I was met at the gate by the whole family – my two aunts, Mary and Ersilia, my uncle Ray, my cousins, John and Donald, my siblings, David and Mary, and of course, my mother and father.

My mother was ecstatic, of course, and my father proud and relieved that I had returned unharmed from the war. I felt a little sheepish about the war, as I felt my experience paled in comparison to both my father's and my uncle's service in WWII. My father had commanded a Sherman tank in the Battle of the Bulge, as well as other places, and my uncle was a 40 mm anti-aircraft gun mount captain on an aircraft carrier in the Pacific in the worst of the kamikaze period.

Author's Note: In fact, it was my father's unit (Combat Command B/7th Armored Division), moving quickly

---

* *The money I was given, in the form of a check, was my "mustering out" pay, by which the military squares with you financially, and in so doing, indicates that it is more or less done with you.*

from Holland to the Belgian town of St. Vith, who, at
terrible expense, blunted the main German advance and
held off Hitler's best units for a critical week, thus buy-
ing time for the much heralded Patton to arrive and re-
lieve the much honored and publicized "band of broth-
brothers" at Bastogne. But that's a story for another day.

It seems like the punch line of an old joke, but soon after I left for Viet Nam, my parents moved. Unlike the butt of the old joke, my parents told me where they moved to. After meeting me at the airport, they took me to my new home in the new Aurora sub-division of Boulder Hill and the family reunion continued.

The next day was Sunday and the three sisters cooked a welcome home spaghetti dinner, made from scratch in the old-style, and it was terrific. To top it off, my best friend Vern was invited to join us and I was happy to be re-united with those I most cared about. What a great day – my family, my best friend, and my mother's (and my aunt's) cooking. I was truly home at last. At least for now.

Acknowledgments

I want to thank my family, and my friends over the years, without whom I would have had nothing to write. I also want to thank all of the artists and writers who gave me the music, and other works, which I refer to as the soundtrack of my life, which have brought back to me many of the memories which this book recounts. In particular, those listed below, whose words I have included in some of those stories.

MOMENTS TO REMEMBER
by Al Stillman and Robert Allen
Published by Larry Spier Music LLC, New York, NY.
Printed with permission. All rights reserved.

WAND'RIN' STAR (from *Paint Your Wagon*)
Words by ALAN JAY LERNER
Music by FREDERICK LOEWE
Copyright © 1951 (Renewed) ALAN JAY LERNER and
FREDERICK LOEWE
Publication and Allied Rights Assigned to
CHAPPELL & CO., INC.
All Rights Reserved
Used By Permission of ALFRED MUSIC